D1321953

WRITING
WORKSHOP
NOTEBOOK

Notes on creating
and workshopping

•

Alan Ziegler

SOUVENIR PRESS

KENSINGTON & CHELSEA LIBRARIES SERVICE	
Askews	
808.02 ZIE	
	PO-24200

Copyright © 2008 by Alan Ziegler

First published in the USA by Soft Skull Press,
An Imprint of Counterpoint LLC

Brief portions of this book were adapted from Creative Writing in America, Journal of a Living Experiment, Teachers & Writers magazine, and The Writing Workshop Volumes I and II.

First published in Great Britain in 2008 by Souvenir Press Ltd
43 Great Russell Street, London WC1B 3PD

The right of Alan Ziegler to be identified as the author of this work has been asserted by him in accordance with the Copyright, Designs and Patents Act, 1988

All rights reserved. No part of this publication may be reproduced, stored in a retrieval system or transmitted, in any form or by any means, electronic, mechanical, photocopying, or otherwise, without the prior permission of the Copyright owner.

ISBN 9780285638266

Printed and bound in Great Britain by
MPG Books Ltd, Bodmin, Cornwall

to my students

ACKNOWLEDGMENTS

My enormous gratitude to: Barbara Thimm for her astute comments on two drafts of this manuscript; Richard Locke for so very much; Binnie Kirshenbaum, who pointed me in the direction of Soft Skull; Richard Nash, who epitomizes all that is wonderful and essential about independent publishing; Leslie Woodard, whose prodigious teaching talent is matched by her spirit; Thom Blaylock, Kara Levy, and Shahid Naeem for their notes; all the colleagues who have enriched my thinking about writing and teaching, including Nick Bozanic, Lucie Brock-Broido, Nicole Burdette, Loren-Paul Caplin, Lacy Crawford, Leo Hamalian, Jocelyn Harvey, Dennis Hayes, Leslie Price Hayes, Richard Howard, J.R. Humphreys, Paul Langston, Eric Lerner, Phillip Lopate, Ben Marcus, Robert Montgomery, David Plante, Patty O'Toole, Phyllis Raphael, Dale Worsley, and Bill Zavatsky, among many others; and Erin, as always.

My deepest thanks to all those Columbia University students whose unattributed words I have included from class utterances, marginalia on manuscripts, journals, and anonymous evaluations.

CONTENTS

CONTENTS

Contents

note \nōt\ A brief written observation, record, or abstract of facts, *esp.* one intended to aid the memory, or to serve as a basis for a more complete statement or for future action.

—Oxford English Dictionary

PREFACE

Books on writing proliferate; why did I write one more? I was impelled by a familiar confluence of reasons: The writing workshop is something I know and want to know more about; I care about how we relate to our own and others' writing; I want to have a felicitous impact on the reader's experience with writing and critiquing. And, I want someone I don't know to say: "I liked reading this."

That's why I wrote the book. Why should you read it? I hope you will find it useful: if you are taking (or thinking of taking) a writing workshop; if you are a workshop teacher; if you are a solitary writer (a workshop-of-one). And, no matter who you are, I hope at times you will think: I like reading this.

My initial plan was to focus on the workshop experience, but I couldn't do that without dealing with the heart that sustains the workshop's brain: the act of creation. Thus, Part One is concerned with the work that leads to the drafts on the workshop table, and Part Two emphasizes what happens when these drafts are critiqued. I have drawn many of the quotes and anecdotes from creative fields outside of writing.

Teachers of writing do not open up cans of lectures. Pedagogy in workshops gets doled out in brief exegeses, often opportunistically as the work comes across the table. I have adapted this process by arranging the book into notes, which you can read sequentially or alight on as you flip through the pages. While each note is self-contained, there is purposeful overlap and reinforcement among them. I had a gym teacher whose mantra was "Gotta know the fundamentals," and he would keep reminding us of them. In writing—as in sports—the fundamentals remain the same no matter how advanced one is.

Like most workshop teachers, I have learned—even earned—the ability to speak with authority about writing. But I often feel like Jean-Jacques Beineix, the director of *Diva*, when he said, "I feel like I'm playing at being a director. I size things up, arch my brow and say, 'No, not exactly. That's, ahem, not quite right.'"

Just as Beineix is likely to be correct when he says that a setup or a take isn't "quite right," I usually know where a student's poem or story is lacking (and how it might be improved). But it is always possible that I am wrong, so I hear in my own voice a quivering undertone. Because I am the author of this and two previous books on writing workshops, you may tend to read what I write as being authoritative. I could have put an "ahem" in each sentence, but it's easier if you occasionally imagine that quiver, like a tiny hop on a polygraph line—one so subtle that the examiner declares the test inconclusive: "He's not outright lying, but he's nervous about *something*."

Almost all writers get nervous, if not when they write, then when they invite others to comment on their writing. This is the boat we are all in. I offer this book with the hope that it leads to smoother sailing.

INTRODUCTION

"Can writing really be taught?"

I have been asked this question many times after revealing what I do for a living. Maybe I should find out where the questioner works and respond: "Can the law really be practiced?" or "Doesn't the car sell itself? Instead, I offer wimpy (but true) answers like:

"Sort of, by accelerating the discovery process."

"You don't so much teach it—you provoke it."

"You discuss the tools of the trade and how to use them."

"You instill students with the courage to write and to expose their writing to scrutiny."

One day I will splurge and declare, "Yes, indeed, it can!"

But perhaps the real question is: "Can writing be *learned*?"

"It depends on the learner" is the wimpy answer, but I say with confidence that the writing workshop *facilitates* learning, and it may even be necessary for some writers at some point in their development, though it is never sufficient.

Heuristic (which shares its Greek root with *eureka*) is a helpful concept in thinking about writing and responding to writing. A heuristic procedure is an informed method of trial-and-error—a strategy, not a recipe. Mathematician George Polya's 1945 book *How to Solve It* popularized heuristic as a method for problem solving, placing value on such notions as determination and discipline ("Willpower is needed that can outlast years of toil and bitter disappointments") along with more concrete strategies (such as asking, "Did you use all the data?" and "Do you know a related problem?").

What I love about heuristic is its lack of absolutism. In this book I do not offer rigid protocols guaranteed to produce successful pieces of writing, but rather a buffet of tacks (to be tempered by instinct) for composition, revision, and critique. The suggestions and templates for writing and workshopping in this book can be thought of as heuristics you can adopt or adapt to work for you.

This book is not The Way, but it might help point you in the direction of Your Way.

PART ONE

Notes on Creating

A voice comes to one in the dark. Imagine.

—opening of *Company* by Samuel Beckett

I

Notes on:
The Work

It's a privilege to muck about in sentences all morning...
You don't do it from willpower; you do it from an
abiding passion for the field.

— Annie Dillard

Prefatory Note: Why Bother?

Writing can be such a bother, so why bother? You wouldn't have this book in your hands if you really needed a detailed answer, but it never hurts to remind ourselves:

We write because there are stories we must tell, or because we must tell stories.

We write to remember; we write to forget.

We write to create something that wasn't there before; we write to re-create (and likely transform) something that was.

We write for sheer pleasure: the pen gliding, halting, then gliding again across the page; the clicking of keys projecting words on the screen; the typewriter ribbon palpating the paper. Boris Pasternak describes his early work: "To write those poems, to cross out, revise, and correct them and then rewrite them again, was something that I felt to be an absolute necessity and gave me immense pleasure that brought me to the verge of tears."

We write for the sense of a healing pain, the pain of a massage on a sore muscle. As Aristotle says, "Objects which in themselves we view with pain, we delight to contemplate when reproduced with minute fidelity."

We write to move the reader in the heart and mind, or to change the reader in some way—if only to imbue greater appreciation for the moon or a cup of coffee.

We write to be called a bastard: I once sent a book of my poetry to an old friend, who responded to one of my "lost love" poems with a note saying, "Jesus, I thought I was over her. The memories you stirred with that poem . . ." He closed with, "You bastard." It pleased me "to the verge of tears."

Yes, writing has its pitfalls and pratfalls. Dorothy Parker (among others) has been quoted as saying that she hates writing but loves having written. I was a bit milder when I used to tell classes (thinking I was the first), "I don't always like writing, but I love having written." Now, more and more, I cherish the act of writing as its own reward. I try not to focus on the value of my creations so much that I lose touch with the joy *of* creation. The opinions of others and the occasional attendant perks remain coveted, but are not essential.

Now I can say that I write because I love writing, even if I don't always like what I have written.

Scribblers and Mush

When I was in my mid-twenties, through some unmapped perambulations I found myself holding a masters in creative writing, co-editing a literary magazine, and being a poet in the schools. Not every poem or story I sent out was attached to a boomerang. A friend asked me what my plans were, and I told him about an upcoming reading and teaching gig. He frowned and said, "No, I mean your future. If you think this is going to be your life, you're living in a fool's paradise!" That sounded pretty damn good, and my career choice was settled.

Still, it was years before I felt comfortable with the honorific "writer." ("Fool" set the bar so much lower.) The primary definition of *writer* is one who writes "especially as an occupation or profession." This can be intimidating. I introduced a student to a colleague as a "writer," and she said, "Oh no, not yet." She was concerned that people would hold her work to a higher standard and that she might be judged by such signposts of success as publications and readings.

I take photographs and tell jokes, but I wouldn't dare call myself a photographer or a comedian, which would be an invitation to a comeuppance. If you tell someone "I am a poet," the response could be, "No, you're not," but if you say, "I write poems," no one can riposte, "No, you don't." In his memoir *A Storyteller's Story*, Sherwood Anderson refers to writers as "scribblers." I like that—who would want to shoot down a humble scribbler?

Whether you think of yourself as a writer, a scribbler, or a student, ultimately it is not about what you call yourself; it's about how you think. In *The Paper Chase*, John Houseman's Professor Kingsfield declaims in his stentorian voice: "You teach yourselves the law, but I train your mind. You come in here with a skull full of mush, and you leave thinking like a lawyer." His point is that it is not enough to know the law—you have to know how to think about it. Likewise, thinking like a writer goes beyond knowing linguistic rules and regulations.

If Professor Kingsfield taught writing, he might say, "You will leave here, as you came in, with your skull full of mush. But you'll know how to organize that mush. You'll know how to transform it. You'll know how to gather more mush to be organized and transformed. You'll leave thinking like a writer!"

Gestation

Writers spend a lot of writing-time not writing, and that's not a bad thing. Sometimes we need to put off putting words on the page because the material is percolating, not yet strong enough to pour. It is not procrastination to wait for the tea to steep or, on a more grandiose scale, to wait nine months before delivering the baby. Nourishment must be provided before new life meets the eyes of the world; in creative work, gestation takes place behind the mind's curtain as we cogitate, dream, daydream, and read.

John Steinbeck devoted years of mental gestation to *East of Eden*. "It has been planned a long time. I planned it when I didn't know what it was about," he wrote as he embarked on a year writing the book "I have always wanted and have worked and prayed to be able to write." Over a period of six months, George Eliot consulted more than two hundred books on Italian life before starting to write her historical novel *Romola*.

I used to write in a café called The Balcony on New York's Upper West Side (with a life-size mannequin of Genet's Madam Irma on the balcony above the bar). Another writer was there almost every afternoon, reading and jotting notes. After about a year, he told me, "Now I am ready to begin the novel."

If you are taking a workshop, you don't have expanses of prep time, but you can allocate some of the time you do have to gestation.

Time Off

What if you just can't get going—if you have genuine writer's block, and the words that do make it to the page are inert? How long do you plow an arid field?

Here's one prescription: take a week off, absolutely no writing! (Unless, of course, you have an assignment due.)

During your week off, you can do some writerly reading—reading as a form of writing instruction rather than research. Select a piece from a writer you admire, and read it straight through. Try not to be intimidated by the writing; remember, you are reading a polished product. Reread it several times (if it's a novel, select excerpts), focusing with each read-through on one aspect of the writer's craft, such as description, dialogue, exposition, use of adjectives and adverbs, or time management. As Vladimir Nabokov writes, you "should notice and fondle details." For poetry, examine line-breaks, imagery, and diction (including word elisions).

How are surprises and revelations set up? Reread the beginning in light of the ending, and vice versa. Transcribe exemplary passages—as Gertrude Stein was preparing to write her first novel, she copied parts of *The Wings of a Dove* into her notebook. Glean at least one "lesson" about writing that you could articulate to fellow writers, such as how the author manages shifting points of view or utilizes dialogue for exposition.

A former student confessed that she hadn't written in a year. I told her about a writer who announced his *intention* not to write for a year in order to smooth out the ruts in his brain, allowing new material to take shape. He lasted a month, and his work took off. "And you were able to do the *whole year*," I said to my student. "Congratulations. I can't wait to see what happens."

Yes, that was a con job (it had not been her intention to abstain from writing), but "con" is an abbreviation of *confidence*, which should join inspiration and perspiration as elements that spur creativity. I was trying to instill confidence in her by pointing out how her dry spell could reap rewards.

A few weeks later, my blocked student gave me a folder of

fragments, frustrated that no single piece had taken hold. My response was: "I see related images and themes. Flesh them out and give them an overall title. I think you have the makings for a portfolio of prose poems." She put together a powerful collection, about which she could honestly say, "This took me a year to write."

The Writer as Worker

The "don't-write" strategy can only be used sparingly. What about procrastination that stems from a lack of will or energy? You long for a stretch of open highway to follow through on your ideas, but when the traffic clears, the engine stalls. You feel a little like Charles Baudelaire's description of Samuel Cramer in *La Fanfarlo*: "The sun of laziness which incessantly glows within him vaporizes and destroys the half measure of genius that Heaven has bestowed on him."

"Rewriting is writing" goes the adage, but *writing must always precede rewriting*, no matter how it gets done. Think of yourself as a working writer. It's a job. You wouldn't have the option of waiting for inspiration if you were working a diner grill during breakfast rush with the manager lurking and hungry customers glaring from the counter. The eggs can go over easy or hard, but they are going over. Your job as a writer is to throw down the words and attend to them until they are done. Punch in and get to work. Take your coffee breaks, but don't stray too far from the grill until your shift is done. (Periodically pacing the room counts as working.) Maintain a time card if it helps.

Isn't this a sacrilege against the holy act of writing? Shouldn't you care more about your writing than about flipping eggs? Of course, but it's all part of the confidence game. Sometimes, caring too much leads to writer's block. You may have to play a role and pretend to stop caring.

Or, try another sacrilege: you don't really want to be a good writer writing a good story. Think: *I am a bad writer engaged to write a bad story. The only way I can start is with a bad sentence. . . . I just wrote a bad sentence, so I'm right on track. I can move on to my next bad sentence.* When you are finished, close with Milly Bloom's P.S. to a letter in James Joyce's *Ulysses*: "Excuse bad writing, am in a hurry. Byby." (Indeed, have a rubber stamp made of this quote and put it on everything you write before you show it to someone.)

If the bad-writer persona doesn't suit you, then try the great-writer mantra: *I am a world-famous writer whose sheer talent allows me to write no wrong. . . . I just wrote a fabulous sentence, and now I can't help but write another one.*

Once you have written, you can attend to the writing that is rewriting.

Good Times

What will you say when an interviewer or someone from the audience at a reading asks you: "Do you write every day? At the same time?"

John Milton felt that the early morning was the friendliest time for the Muses. He would have a stock of verses ready to dictate when his amanuensis arrived, and if his amanuensis was late, Milton would complain that he "wanted to be milked." Charles Darwin was also a morning writer and often announced with satisfaction around noon: "*I've* done a good day's work." Anthony Trollope's practice was "to be at my table every morning at 5:30 a.m." and "complete my literary work before I dressed for breakfast."

Others write while the Miltons, Darwins, and Trollopes sleep. Gustave Flaubert might start at 4 p.m. and work deep into the night. Kafka had a day job (which he probably thought was *something*-esque) and also wrote surrounded by darkness. On the night he wrote "The Judgment," he last looked at the clock at 2 a.m.; when the maid arrived—with the bed "undisturbed"—he stretched and declared, "I've been writing until now."

Some writers claim—contrary to visible and auditory evidence—to be working all the time, like Jack Nicholson's character in *The Shining*, who points out rather crudely to his wife that he is working whether or not she hears the typewriter. Others constantly bemoan their lack of productivity yet somehow turn out the work; the writing grows almost imperceptibly, like hairs on the head. One day they've finished a story and need a haircut.

The married writers Shirley Hazzard and Francis Steegmuller had contrasting work styles. Hazzard on Steegmuller: "He goes straight to his desk in the morning and stays there. I wander around. I need a lot of silence in my head to find out what I think." Steegmuller on Hazzard: "I peer in the room and I think she's free; but it's reverie . . . I've had to learn that Shirley's writing when she doesn't look it. She can be tidying up around the house, but she's working." (As far as I know, Hazzard never told her husband, "I'm working whether or not you hear the vacuum cleaner.")

With some writers, you might not only hear that they are working, you might hear *what* they are working on. Allen Ginsberg composed "Wichita Vortex Sutra" into a tape recorder on a car trip, and Richard Powers writes out loud, using voice-recognition software.

Sustained writing sessions are to be coveted but, just as catnaps can be more efficient than nighttime sleep, so can flurries of writing be refreshingly productive. I often take *catwrites* during the day: a few minutes here and there with no warm-up. When inspiration invites, you may need to steal time from something else. Ginsberg delayed going to a party for twenty minutes to write "Sunflower Sutra." He noted: "Me at desk scribbling, Kerouac at cottage door waiting for me to finish so we could go off somewhere party."

While I was in graduate school, one of my strangest and most felicitous writing sessions came out of sheer shyness. My roommate at the time was visited by a musician whose work I admired. From across the room, my roommate introduced me as his "poet friend." Too shy to join the conversation, I reached for my notebook and pen and pretended to be writing. The poem I pretended to write came out almost complete in one draft (in less time than it took Ginsberg to write "Sunflower Sutra"). The poem's central metaphor is self-disappearance; although it is surrealistic, I wrote from experience as the experience was occurring.

Give yourself a modest minimum goal. It can be quantity: Early in his career, Stendhal assigned himself "*Vingt lignes par jour, génie ou pas*" ("Twenty lines a day, genius or not") to guarantee progress as he worked on a book. The novelist Harry Mathews "deliberately mistook his words as a method for overcoming the anxiety of the blank page" for his collection *20 Lines a Day*.

Or, it can be time: Block out thirty minutes a day minimum for writing—any words on any page—four days a week. That's two hours a week, 104 hours a year. The key is to block out time when you have nothing scheduled afterward. On most days you will do more. On any given day you can do less, but you have to make up that time before the end of the week.

The poet David Ignatow wrote in his journal: "I am tired and I would like to lie down but deliberately I keep myself seated here to write, no matter what. The idea is to write to make the gesture, to say something worth saying that can send me to bed happy." With this in mind, many years ago I created the *Tonight Show* Approach as a way to send myself to bed happy. After Johnny Carson's monologue, I would mute the sound as Johnny swung his invisible golf club, then write until Johnny thanked his guests. These days, *Law and Order* reruns work well. I start writing with the discovery of the body and stop with the verdict. If I am pressed for time, I can end my session with the arraignment.

Workspace

If you have a job at a factory or office, the workspace is provided for you. Most writers are self-deployed and must provide for themselves. Where to write? Lord Byron wrote *Don Juan* in Venice at a window overlooking the Grand Canal. Most of us aren't that lucky (he also had fourteen servants, a monkey, a peacock, and an Egyptian crane).

You can create a suite of offices in one room. Edmund Wilson worked on several projects at the same time, each on a separate desk. Instead of moving papers, he moved himself. W.B. Yeats laid out his work on a large deal table. If you are space-limited, part of your floor can serve as a deal table. Keep it organized if you can, but if you can't you will be in good company. While working on *Nightwood*, Djuna Barnes wrote in a letter that "the whole damned floor is a mess of it, no table big enough to spread it all out on, so I crawl about on the floor."

Writers vary in their preferred temperatures. Some find that cool air keeps the blood flowing, while Flaubert worked well in the heat, which had "the effect of brandy." When you are having trouble writing, try opening or closing a window.

If you don't have the coveted room of one's own (preferably in a clean, well-lighted place), you can transform part of your living space into a writing office. Park your laptop and hang a shingle. Let anyone you live with know that this is your study; invisible walls can be respected as much as closed doors.

Work in someone else's room. Even before the days of laptops, handhelds, and telepathic digital scribes (which I assume will be on the market by the time this book gets out), writers worked in public spaces. Hemingway wrote in the *Closerie de Lilas* in Paris, equipped with blue-backed notebooks, pencils, and a pencil sharpener on a marble-topped table. The pencil sharpener was his nod to technology (using a pocket knife was too wasteful for serious writing). Oh, he also carried a horse chestnut and a real rabbit's foot (with its fur worn off) in his right pocket for luck. I don't require an animal sacrifice, but I do value special small objects as amulets for writing: miniature typewriters, a magnifying glass from a flea market in London, a silver hand-clip from a shop on Rue Bonaparte in Paris.

If you are torn between the sensory input of the café and the solitude of the garret, you can have both by writing at home until you run out of steam and then relocating to a café. If you live in a city, you can keep moving your writing feast to the next corner and the next café. No matter how you feel about Starbucks and the like, they have become havens for the laptop brigade. As a bonus, you might gather some material by discreet eavesdropping.

The work doesn't have to be sedentary. Try some choreography, like Vladimir Mayakovsky, who reported: "I walk along, waving my arms and mumbling almost wordlessly, now shortening my steps so as not to interrupt my mumbling, now mumbling more rapidly in time with my steps." (Perhaps this kind of behavior is why writers tend to congregate in big cities.) According-ing to Mark Van Doren, John Berryman "walked with verse as if in a trance" while a student at Columbia.

You don't have to be the one doing the moving. Bob Dylan suggests, "You can write a song anywhere, in a railroad compartment, on a boat, on horseback—it helps to be moving." Frank O'Hara wrote "Poem" ("Lana Turner has collapsed!") on the Staten Island Ferry traveling to a reading at Wagner College. I especially like writing in my corner office at the back of a New York City bus. I know the work is going well when I miss my stop.

"And Away We Go"

Some writers need the Ed Norton approach to start writing. On *The Honeymooners*, Art Carney's Ed couldn't just sit down at the piano and play; he would stretch his fingers, crack his knuckles, and dance with his arms. Your warm-up routine might be to grind the beans and brew the coffee, adjust the chair, rearrange books on the shelf, check email.

If this goes on too long, imagine Jackie Gleason's Ralph Kramden bellowing, "Cam on!!!" and jolt yourself into beginning.

The chair of a committee I was on—a chemist by trade—was leading a routine meeting when an unexpected suggestion was made. "I've been in mechanical mode," he responded. "I'd better get into operational mode." I wasn't familiar with the terminology, but I understood the distinction. If I am not in the mood to write, I might promise myself that I am just going to do some mechanical-mode tasks, such as entering handwritten notes and revisions into the computer. Usually, I will click into operational mode. From such broken promises work gets done.

You not only need the wherewithal to start something, but also the will to keep going. I watched a master dance class taught by the choreographer Bella Lewitsky, during which she asked students to execute a series of steps from one end of the dance floor to the other. Whenever a student faltered and lapsed into a sheepish gait, Lewitsky would command, "Finish the line."

Sometimes when I am writing, I get befuddled or dispirited and want to sneak away, but I tell myself, "Finish the line."

And when I have finished the line, I add: "Now, on to the next one!"

Not Knowing

The act of creation is often a quest rather than a re-quest. In Kenneth Patchen's final interview, he talks about "a quality of searching, of clumsiness in the craft almost like Van Gogh, for example, whose breaking with tradition seems almost as though he didn't know what to do next. And I think this is the stance of the creator."

I crossed paths with the poet Gerald Stern, who spent a couple of days at the Interlochen Arts Academy when I was writer-in-residence. Over lunch, I gave him a book of my poetry, and at dinner he had some nice things to say about it. He especially liked a poem that I had added to the manuscript out of fondness though I wasn't sure it would hold up to critical scrutiny. I asked Stern why he liked the poem—hoping he would articulate some literary quality to support my fondness for it—and he replied, "Because I got the feeling you didn't know what the hell you were doing." I felt affirmed, and this attitude has helped me spawn many subsequent pieces. I treasure the luscious feeling I get when I don't know what the hell I am doing but I really want to keep doing it.

During a hospital stay after a head injury, Jorge Luis Borges was afraid to write poetry—which had been his primary form—

because failure could confirm that he had not fully recovered his "mental integrity." He decided to minimize the risk by writing short stories. Borges later told an interviewer, "If it hadn't been for that particular knock on the head I got, perhaps I would never have written short stories." He didn't know what the hell he was doing. But look what he did.

Poetic Delirium

Good writings happen to those who wait. Children's author Enid Blyton wrote to Peter McKellar—who was researching *Imagination and Thinking*—that she has "merely to open the sluice gates" and, with her portable typewriter on her knee, wait with a blank mind: "The story is enacted in my mind's eye almost as if I had a private cinema screen there . . . I am in the happy position of being able to write a story and read it for the first time . . . Sometimes a character makes a joke . . . and I think, 'Well, I couldn't have thought of that myself in a hundred years!' And then I think, 'Well, who *did* think of it then?'"

The answer, of course, is: *She* did.

Sometimes you don't even need to wait at your keyboard. Rather than putting nose to the grindstone, you merely need the fortitude to put nose to the pillow. Mayakovsky tried for two days to come up with an image "to describe the tenderness a lonely man feels for his only love" (evidently, not even dancing in the streets worked this time). He went to bed on the third night with a headache. During the night he "leapt out of bed half-awake" with the image of how much a crippled soldier "cherishes his one leg." In the dim light of a match, he wrote on a cigarette packet: "his one leg." When morning came, Mayakovsky puzzled for two hours over the phrase, wondering "how it had got there."

The answer, again, is: *He* put it there.

Unconscious material can rise to the top even when you are not waiting or sleeping, like an evasive song lyric or the dog's name in the *Thin Man* movies (I'll spare you: it was Asta). Mental knots often loosen spontaneously when you step away from the task. I was grappling with the title of a story, and the best I could come up with was "God's Work," which was close but no cigar—it didn't illuminate the entryway into the story. I closed the file on my computer. While checking the five-day weather forecast for a place I was to visit in six days, it came to me: "God's Will." Cigar.

Writers spend countless hours looking for the precise word, the transcendent image, the felicitous turn of narrative: Doesn't it feel good when these things just come to us? The rub is that the chance of a spontaneous solution can be in direct proportion to the amount of conscious work we have been doing. In getting your writing to soar, there is no such thing as a free launch.

The surrealists' notion that art and literature stem directly from the unconscious is quite appealing: just remove the lid of conscious effort and let your "automatic" pilot take over. For me, Vicente Huidobro was closer to the mark when he wrote about reason's role in organizing *poetic delirium*: "If reason and imagination do not work in unison, one or both will suffocate."

Baudelaire writes about "genius" as being childhood recaptured with "the analytical mind that enables it to bring order into the sum of experience, involuntarily amassed." And Max Jacob states it eloquently: "Lyricism belongs to the unconscious, but an unconscious under supervision."

With the unconscious doing so much of the work, the least we can do is supervise.

*   *   *

The admixture of hard work (laboring over one's writing) and dream work (reveling in poetic delirium) may sound contradictory, as does much advice you hear about writing. It serves well to embrace these contradictions in the spirit of F. Scott Fitzgerald's dictum that "the test of a first-rate intelligence is the ability to hold two opposed ideas in the mind at the same time, and still retain the ability to function." (A note of caution: Fitzgerald wrote this in an essay titled "The Crack-Up.")

Keeping Going – A Note on Process

One way to keep the work flowing is to be acquainted with the writing process. Researchers have confirmed what writers have always known: most writing is done in stages, and the stages are often repeated, not necessarily in order. Here is one model for this recursive process.

Prewrite: Notate, vegetate, cogitate.

Exploratory draft: Ragged and reckless, no stopping for red lights.

Developmental draft: Shaping and amplifying.

Revision for you: Am I saying what I want to say?

Revision for others: Will the reader know what I am saying?

Tidying up: Punctuation, grammar, spelling.

Writers constantly ease or jolt from one mode to another. You are revising one idea when another comes to mind, necessitating a shift to exploratory drafting. Or, you write early drafts with abandon and revise with tranquility, but after tidying up you return to gut instinct to undo or redo passages.

Be careful not to turn process into procedure. Use the writing process as a backbone but maintain a free spirit. You can polish the life out of that rare, brilliant early draft (lucky you).

And, even though it is not protocol to worry about spelling and the like until the end of the process, sometimes I just can't continue with a first draft until I check a fact or look up a definition. (Perhaps I need a break to allow my unconscious to loosen a knot.)

The computer is a wonderful tool for writers, but it can blur the way we experience the process. Drafts produced with a computer tend not to be as discrete as they are with a typewriter or pen. By constantly deleting, cutting, and pasting on the screen, you may wind up with a final draft without any record of an entire previous version. Save each piece occasionally under different names so that you can consult earlier drafts.

As you revise, don't refer only to the most recent draft, sentencing all previous excisions and alterations to oblivion. Something may look better now than it did when you changed it. Or perhaps something that didn't work before now succeeds in light of subsequent revisions. Prior to writing a final draft, have an *appeals session*, reviewing earlier decisions. Force yourself to re-key a piece from scratch at least once. You will likely find yourself making changes through your hands that you might not have conceived with just your eyes on the text.

With all the emphasis on process and revision, what about Jack Kerouac's "spontaneous prose" ("Never afterthink to 'improve' or defray impressions") and "First thought, best thought," the notion Allen Ginsberg adopted from his teacher Chogyam Trungpa? Such spontaneity didn't work for Flaubert, whose first thoughts left him with "monstrous negligences," which he overlaid with revision after revision. Can our "first-rate intelligence" cope with these seemingly opposed approaches?

Sure. Not everyone needs to work the same way. If spontaneous composition with little revision works for you, fine, but you're probably in the minority. Even Ginsberg emphasized that access to the spontaneous mind requires intense mental training, and he cautioned students that "first thought" doesn't mean "first cheap remark" or "talk-babble to the self." And, as Douglas Brinkley points out, Kerouac's legendary three-week binge typing *On the Road* on a continuous scroll was "the outcome of a fastidious process of outlining, chapter drafting, and trimming."

Even first thoughts that *are* the best usually need to be revised as you translate from thought to written language. Playfully, I can even imagine Trungpa's *first* thought being, "The first idea—no, image; no, thought—that occurs to you may be the very best you can ever come up with," before he sculpted it into "First thought, best thought."

Dante Gabriel Rossetti writes that William Blake "was wont to affirm—'First thoughts are best in art, second thoughts in other matters,'" yet at the Metropolitan Museum of Art I stared, spellbound, at a handwritten manuscript on which Blake had replaced *form* with *frame* in "The Tyger." I guess he thought, "On second thought: *frame.*"

To make it even more interesting: The expectation that you will revise with care may provide you with the "cover" you need to write without inhibition on a first draft, allowing you to get at those first thoughts that *are* indeed best. Charles Darwin notes in his autobiography: "Formerly I used to think about my sentences before writing them down; but for several years I have found that it saves time to scribble in a vile hand whole pages as quickly as I possibly can, contracting half the words; and then correct deliberately. Sentences thus scribbled down are often better ones than I could have written deliberately."

A new dictum: *Vile hand, best hand.*

Stopping

Did you ever work up a nice head of steam on skates or a bicycle only to realize that stopping might be a problem? Sometimes it is easier to pick up a piece than it is to let it go, not sure if you have brought the work to appropriate closure and fine-tuned the language to hit the right notes.

Colonel Green in the movie *Bridge on the River Kwai* could be speaking to writers when he says, "As I've told you before, in a job like yours, even when it's finished, there's always one more thing to do." When Leo Tolstoy was proofreading the galleys for periodical installments of *Anna Karenina*, he would make so many emendations that his wife had to stay up all night copying the changes with her clear handwriting. The next morning, Tolstoy would find a pristine pile and, according to his son Ilya, carry the sheets "off to his study to have 'just one last look.'" By evening, "the whole thing" had been rewritten. The next day, Tolstoy would say, "There's just one bit I want to look through again," but he would "recast the whole thing afresh." Eventually even Tolstoy moved on.

When I was a newspaper reporter, I kept tinkering with a feature story until my editor blew the deadline whistle. He swooped by and lifted the papers off my desk, looked at my bereft expression, and said gently, "Sometimes you just have to stop."

When your laboring becomes belaboring but you are reluctant to let go, it may be time to stop—at least long enough to take it to the workshop.

Slow Writers

Don't measure your output only in quantitative terms. *Work* is defined as "force times distance," and you may have to exert a lot of force to go a short linear distance. You can accomplish the same amount of work producing one difficult page or ten easy ones. Flaubert spent five days working on one page of *Madame Bovary*. I'd say it was a good week's work.

It takes skill to work slowly. When I was in graduate school, a classmate complained, "I wrote for five hours today and only got one paragraph."

I replied: "I'm not a good enough writer yet to do that."

The Writer as Explorer

Writers, like explorers, don't make the same trip twice. You may know where you intend to go but not how to get there. (A mission isn't necessarily a failure if you wind up somewhere else; Columbus didn't complete his assignment, but he has a Day.) Or, you may have no specific destination in mind as you set off to find what there is to be found.

This doesn't mean that you start each writing journey with a blank slate. You constantly adapt what you have learned from previous journeys, cutting through mental thickets with ever-sharpening instincts. You draw on a mélange of skills and attitudes, tempered with experience and optimism.

Like jazz musicians, we improvise as we apply heart to technique. A guitarist once dazzled me with an intricate array of chords and single-note runs. I asked him what he had just done, and he was able to reconstruct an approximation of his improvisation, playing slowly while narrating the chord progressions, resolutions, tempi, and harmonies. His narration *followed* each move; he was transcribing what had come naturally. He had not been aware of what he was doing *while* he was doing it, but any listener would have concluded: "This guy knows what he's doing."

Some artists create spontaneously, without study, and, unlike that guitarist, would not be able to explain what they do in technical terms. Then there are the rest of us. We write, read, workshop, write, and read some more. We develop an array of techniques and strategies that can constitute an *approach*. Any approach you develop should be flexible and, at any given time, disposable. You don't want to travel empty-handed, but neither do you want to be loaded down—how are you going to pick up anything new?

We become the experienced explorer, finding an element of the familiar in everything foreign, feeling a cautious confidence with each new terrain: *I have never made this trip before, but I know how to go places.*

On our best days we fluidly execute complicated narrative and imagistic maneuvers that we can only explicate in retrospect, if at all; we might need the help of smart readers to fully comprehend what we have done. One of the most exhilarating comments I received as a workshop student was: "Wow, I could write an essay about this poem."

Please do, I thought, *I'd love to read it.*

The Doubting Companion

Do you sometimes get an inkling to write, only to stop yourself by thinking, *Nah, it won't be any good?*

I have no advice on how to answer the question *"Will it be good?"* The bad news is that there is no way to know.

The good news is: the very question is no good.

Kurt Vonnegut used to start off our graduate school workshop by asking us what problems we were having with our writing, other than not having enough time. The number one response was some version of self-doubt. Approach your writing with respectful fearlessness. Adopt Miles Davis's attitude: "I never think about not being able to do anything. I just pick up my horn and play the hell out of it."

If you follow only one piece of advice in this book, let it be: Don't ask yourself for permission to write based on the promise that something good will emerge. Don't take *"Nah"* for an answer. Just write the hell out of it.

Doubt and temporary failure are the artist's companions; they should be recognized, listened to, and overruled. For most, doubt never departs, and failure rarely stays away for long. Consider this comment by John Steinbeck: "Although sometimes I have felt that I held fire in my hands and spread a page with shining—I have never lost the weight of clumsiness, of ignorance, of aching inability."

Join Steinbeck and these other doubters:

Walker Percy wrote to Shelby Foote: "I've been in a long spell of accedie, anomie and aridity in which, unlike the saints who writhe under the assaults of devils, I simply get sleepy and doze off." (Of course, no one truly in a state of accedie, anomie, and aridity could write this.)

"Beset with technical difficulties and doubts," Nabokov was carrying the first chapters of *Lolita* to the garden incinerator when fortunately his wife, Vera, stopped him. (I imagine her cajoling, "Vladimir! Don't take out the garbage!")

The great actor Charles Laughton was plagued by self-doubt, especially during the 1937 filming of *I, Claudius*, which was never completed. Laughton would put his head in co-star Merle Oberon's lap and weep, "I can't find my character. I can't find the man." Years later, one of the other actors lamented that Laughton "needed sun and got frost" from the director. Laughton shows enough flashes of brilliance in the surviving footage to make the case that much was lost because no one did for *I, Claudius* what Vera Nabokov would do for *Lolita.*

I witnessed a conversation in the late 1960s between Allen Ginsberg and the painter Arnold Bittleman. Bittleman was describing how he would often paint deep into the night, look admiringly at his work, and go to bed convinced that he had created a great work of art—only to wake up and discover someone must have broken in and ruined his painting. Ginsberg replied that he used to feel that way, but now, even as he is writing, he'll think: "This is the same old bleeeecchhh."

John Berryman didn't read reviews until he was thirty-five because, as he puts it, "I had no skin on . . . I was afraid of being killed by some remark."

Francis Williams—who played trumpet with Duke Ellington—started out as a pianist in his hometown, Toledo. Williams thought he was pretty good until he met a local piano player who was so much better that Williams decided to change instruments: how could he succeed in the piano world if he wasn't even the best in the neighborhood? Perhaps Williams made the right decision, but it was for the wrong reason: his neighbor in Toledo happened to be Art Tatum.

Rebuffs Rejected

One way to counterbalance doubt is to consider the reams of ephemeral rejections and rebuffs. Here are just a few:

Edgar Allan Poe's "The Raven" was initially rejected by *Graham's Magazine* (where Poe had been literary editor). The staff assuaged the rejection by taking up a collection of fifteen dollars for him.

In the August 1849 issue of the *North British Review*, James

Lorimer states that he did not finish reading *Wuthering Heights* due to its "pandemonium of low and brutal creatures, who wrangle with each other in language too disgusting for the eye or the ear to tolerate, and unredeemed, so far as we could see, by one single particle either of wit or humour, or even psychological truth." Lorimer predicts that *Wuthering Heights* "will never be generally read."

Writing in the *Atlantic Monthly* in January 1892, Thomas Bailey Aldrich quotes a critic who said that Emily Dickinson might have become a fifth-rate poet "if she had only mastered the rudiments of grammar and gone into metrical training for about fifteen years." Aldrich takes issue with this, damning with the faintest praise: "If Miss Dickinson had undergone the austere curriculum indicated, she would, I am sure, have become an admirable lyric poet of the second magnitude."

An editor at Editions Ollendorff rejected Marcel Proust's *Remembrance of Things Past* with: "I may be dead from the neck up, but rack my brains as I may, I can't see why a chap should need thirty pages to describe how he turns over in bed before going to sleep." At least the editor raised the possibility that the fault was located above *his* neck rather than Proust's. A Proust supporter responded, "Fortune has knocked at your door and passed you by."

In 1923, a critic for *The Manchester Guardian* compared T. S. Eliot's *The Waste Land* to "waste paper."

William Golding's *Lord of the Flies* was rejected by Jonathan Cape with this painful bit of politeness: "It does not seem to us that you have been wholly successful in working out an admittedly promising idea." Cape referred Golding to another publisher, who also turned it down.

From my own modest experience: I submitted a story to an editor who was an acquaintance; he rejected it. Weeks later I ran into him on the street and he apologized, explaining, "Well,

I didn't love it." (And why did that particular phrase hurt so much? Is it because I'd rather be disliked than not-loved?) I was pleased to respond, "That's all right, *The Paris Review* did."

Robert Burns reacted to a critic with a rhapsodic, vitriolic screed, including: "Thou servile echo of fashionable barbarisms . . . thou carpenter, mortising the awkward joints of jarring sentences . . . thou executioner of construction . . . thou pickled-herring in the puppet-show of nonsense."

Charles Lamb took a long view of rejection: "When my sonnet was rejected, I exclaimed, 'Damn the age; I will write for Antiquity!'"

II

Notes on:
The Material

When material looks good, bite into it. When it bites back, you're on to something. If you're being swallowed, you might have to back off for a while.

It's all about waiting for a fair fight.

Prefatory Note: The Scientific Method

Writing programs tend to be housed in English departments (or, like the program at Columbia, a School of the Arts). But we also have much in common with the sciences, where raw data get collected, sorted, synthesized, analyzed, and often—but not always—turned into something that affects our lives. Like what we do.

Geophysicist Dennis Hayes, in a memoir about research expeditions on a Columbia University ship, quotes his mentor Doc Ewing explaining why the ship was hardly ever in port: "You don't collect much data when your ship is in port, tied to the dock." At sea, Ewing insisted that data be collected around the clock, and Hayes writes that "Ewing was openly criticized by many colleagues for collecting data for which he had no particular use in mind, but he was sure the data contained some valuable information about the Earth that eventually would be useful."

Scientists under Ewing's direction built a "vast data library" before they had the computer hardware and software to do much with it. When the technology caught up, they were "sitting on the mother lode" and "each day seemed to bring an important new discovery."

This section offers some ways to collect a mother lode of data for writing.

Kindling

Great fires start with kindling. Maintain a stockpile of ideas, projects, fragments. Not everything will ignite, but you never know what will.

In his memoirs, Pablo Neruda writes, "I believe in guided spontaneity. For this, the poet must always have some reserves . . . of words, sounds, or images, the ones that buzz right past us like bees. They must be caught quickly and put away in one's pocket." This is easier to know than to do, and Neruda goes on to say, "I am lazy in this respect, but I know I am passing on some good advice."

Once you achieve a critical mass—and keep adding to it— you will always have something to work with, though the material that gets you started on any given piece may, like kindling, burn off after having served its function.

Notebooks

In October 1837, Ralph Waldo Emerson made a felicitous suggestion to a young neighbor, who recounted it in his new notebook: "'What are you doing now?' he asked, 'Do you keep a journal?'—So I make my first entry to-day."

Good thing for Henry David Thoreau—and us—that Emerson asked. I don't know whether Thoreau had heard this suggestion before, but *you* surely have, and you'll hear it again now. Maintain a notebook—indeed, several notebooks of various shapes and sizes (one for the back pocket, one for the book bag, one for the desk, one as a computer file), including at least one special notebook (or a notebook bought in a special place).

You can transform a run-of-the-paper-mill notebook into something special. Jack Kerouac illustrated some of the covers of his spiral pocket notebooks (which he constantly mined for his novels). After seeing photographs of them, I painted some of my notebook covers (a terrific gestation activity).

Notebook writing should be unbound from the chains of perfection quest. Virginia Woolf described her diary writing as "rough & random." Keep your notebooks stocked with dreams, ideas for characters, odd thoughts (someday you may invent odd characters to think them), overheard dialogue, observations, and memories.

Write "nibble notes" (consisting of key words, idea kernels) during the day, instead of counting on a nighttime writing repast that might not happen (too tired, too much in love, or too overwhelmed with how much there is to write). David Ignatow failed to do this on the day he wrote in his journal: "This morning I had an insight into love and self-centeredness, as I walked the street on an errand, and now I can't recall it, pressed by duties at home."

Periodically "save" mental notes into your notebook before your mind's RAM fills up. Flesh out these notes before you forget what they mean. If you do forget, no problem. Mysterious entries detached from context can be transfigured into something more compelling than the original association.

Don't just write about current events. Try to direct your thinking into the past (or future), looking for "spots of time" (as Wordsworth calls them) with "distinct pre-eminence."

Aide-mémoire is a term used in diplomacy for "a written summary or outline of important items of a proposed agreement or diplomatic communication." It also means—less exotically—"an aid to the memory." Think: *Someday I want to write about this, but I don't have the time, energy, and/or perspective now, so I will get down as much as I can in the form of snippets, details, and notes to myself. I can tell instead of show with impunity.*

Sometimes, one can nail it with the *aide-mémoire*. Carolyn Forché's widely anthologized prose poem "The Colonel" started out as a memory that she pared down and rendered "whole, un-lined and as precise as recollection would have it." The text got mixed in with a poetry manuscript. When someone read the manuscript and told Forché, "This is the best one. This is the best poem," she replied, "Oh, no. That's a mistake. That's not a poem." She found out that it is.

Notebook-writing helps allay the fear that the last thing you wrote will be the last thing you will ever write (which is true only once, but let's not go there). The Earth's resources are divided between the renewable (fresh water, timber) and the nonrenew-able (fossil fuels, metals). Some writers fear their creativity is nonrenewable and they may run out of material. But as you cre-ate, seeds get dropped along the way for later cultivation. When you are in a productive groove, your brain often comes up with more than you can handle; keep those seeds in your notebooks for rainy days.

The notebook's value goes beyond being a repository of ma-terial. The very act of memorializing observations, events, and imaginings contributes to the skills integral to one's identity and growth as a writer, just as taking numerous photographs will improve your photographic ability and enable you to see more and see deeper. Virginia Woolf wrote in her diary—about her diary writing—that she could "trace some increase of ease in my professional writing which I attribute to my casual half hours after tea." (Ah, those half hours after tea!)

Self-Important Wheelbarrows

If you have a strong instinct to write something but doubt its importance, apply William Carlos Williams's standard: "But everything in our lives, if it's sufficiently authentic to our lives and touches us deeply enough with a certain amount of feeling, is capable of being organized into a form which can be a poem."

If the material doesn't quite meet this standard, write it anyway. An incident, object, or notion that seems only moderately or peculiarly compelling may become, in the writing, rife with meaning. Indeed, the very act of writing can impart to the reader (as well as to the writer) innate but unnoticed importance. Did Williams *make* red wheelbarrows and cold plums important to us by writing about them? How important was a little island in Lough Gill until Yeats wrote about building a small cabin on "The Lake Isle of Innisfree"? Or Hopper's lighthouses, Cezanne's apples, Monet's water lilies? Would Johnson have been as important without Boswell?

Noble Failures

We all have wished we could go back in time and make something better, given what we know now. You can do this with pieces of writing, but only if you keep track of them. Maintain a folder of deserving pieces that never quite made it. (Sometimes, you don't even have to do much to make a "failed" piece work— it was working all along, and you hadn't realized it.) Robert Lowell dived back into "three incoherent sketches" and "cut, added, and tinkered"; he emerged with "For the Union Dead."

One of my most satisfying writing experiences occurred beside a pool on a spring day in northern Michigan. My friend insisted on going swimming at the Holiday Inn, and I insisted on not going. We compromised: I'd go but not swim. I grabbed my failure-folder and pulled up a chaise next to the deep end.

I came across a short story that an editor had deemed "too sleight rather than too short," adding the cutting trope, "if you catch the difference." Yes, I caught the difference; I just didn't know what to do about it. But there, by the pool, something happened. I filled the margins and interlinear space with notes, words, and arrows. I lost track of time. My friend stopped swimming. I kept writing. The story won an award. Perhaps my friend has a lovely memory of swimming.

What Do You Need to Know and When?

How much do you need to know before you start writing?

Sometimes you just need an impetus, which can be as amorphous as a sensation, a flash of memory, a dream, a phrase. Like a detective, you follow the impetus to see what secrets it might reveal. Jorge Amado told *The New York Times Book Review*, "I'm incapable of imagining a story from beginning to end. I never know what's going to happen next. I just follow where the characters lead me."

It helps to have a strongly felt sense of form, honed through years of reading and writing. (T.S. Eliot once responded facetiously to a reporter's query about the play he was writing: "Why, you see, in the play I study the relations of certain characters with other characters and of certain characters with themselves.") For some writers, any form can get them going. Prior to beginning *Shadow Train*, John Ashbury decided to "write fifty poems of sixteen lines each, so then I knew what I had to do—right? But that doesn't mean it's anything important, or has any profound significance."

Or, you may want to begin with a plan for content, such

as the two-page scenario Flaubert wrote for *Madame Bovary*. In "The Philosophy of Composition," Poe writes that the author should start with the "effect" on the reader and plan right through to the dénouement. He claims that before writing "The Raven," he determined it would be about 100 lines long and require a refrain with a long *o* and an *r* (voila: *Nevermore*). Poe began composing near the end of the poem, "where all works of art should begin." Another writer might not have known there would even be a raven until one came tapping, or what the raven might say until it opened its beak.

Whether you start with an ending or little more than an inkling of a beginning, you should stay open to discoveries along the way. You may find out that you know more than you thought, or that what you thought you knew doesn't hold up to the scrutiny of writing—and you come to know something else.

Originality

If originality is an issue for you, consider W. H. Auden's distinction between *original* and *authentic*: "Some writers confuse authenticity, which they ought always to aim at, with originality, which they should never bother about."

If you do bother about being original, utilize this definition: "Proceeding immediately from its source, or having its source in itself; not arising from or depending on any other thing of the kind; underived, independent." Ask yourself: Did you derive the piece from someone else? Or did it spring up independently?

If the answers are "no" and "yes," then make no apologies. If the answers are "yes" and "no," then you can resort to Ezra Pound's directive and "make it new."

If you can't make it new, make it yours. In Stephen Sondheim's

Sunday in the Park with George, the painter justifies his artistic drought by asserting he has nothing to say "that's not been said," and his companion counters, "Said by *you*?" This is a mantra to write by.

If you eliminate from contention any material that has been handled admirably by so many others, what's left? Such was the dilemma confronted by French poet-composer Blondel de Nesle in this verse: "There's not a word or verse one can think up any more, / no matter how much one picks and chooses, / that hasn't been said and said again/ . . . As for me, I can't keep from singing . . ."

This was composed in the 12th century: before Shakespeare, before Blake, before Dickinson, before Joyce, before Wolfe, Woolf, and Wolfe, before you and me.

If you are still afraid of serving up a cliché, we only have to go back to the 20th century for Pulitzer-Prize winning poet Charles Simic's notebook entry: "The dream of every honest cliché is to enter a great poem." The two key words here are *honest* and *great*. Not easy, but worth aspiring toward.

Within and Without

On a hot summer day, I was standing on the corner of 72nd Street and Broadway in Manhattan. A man in a long black coat ran up to me, stopped short, and implored, "Do you know what happened?"

"Where?" I instinctively replied.

"*Anywhere!*" he shrieked, and ran off.

I assume what he really meant was: "Do you know where to get material for writing?"

"Where?"

"*Anywhere.*"

Your pen or keyboard is the mill, and the whole world is grist. Through writing, you perceive, illuminate, and interpret what goes on internally and externally—as the Beatles sing, "Within you and without you." You look for material with your eyes and mind's eye, and listen with your ears and mind's ear. That's the writer's edge: three eyes and three ears.

You can open yourself to the influence of other writers, but you should never forget to look inward as well. In Sir Philip Sidney's 16th-century sonnet "Loving in Truth," the poet seeks inspiration by "Oft turning others' leaves, to see if thence would flow / Some fresh and fruitful showers upon my sunburned brain," until "helpless in my throes, / Biting my truant pen," he receives this piece of advice: "'Fool,' said my Muse to me, 'look in thy heart, and write.'"

Write what you know is commonly given advice, and fine advice it is, especially for writers who doubt that anything *they* know could be worth writing about. But don't take this to mean, "Don't write what you don't know" or "Only write what you know firsthand."

If I only wrote what I knew firsthand, I would not have written stories from the points of view of an aging ambassador and a touring folk singer; Kafka would not have written *Metamorphosis* or *Amerika* (actually, he didn't—he wrote *The Man Who Disappeared*, which was posthumously named *Amerika* by Max Brod); and Stephen Crane would not have written *The Red Badge of Courage*. Crane eventually did witness real battles, which led him to conclude, with relief, "*The Red Badge* is all right." (If Kafka had made it to the United States, he might have thought otherwise about the accuracy of *Amerika*. *Metamorphosis* is another story.)

Let's amend the adage:

Write what you know; write what you know intuitively; write what you would like to know; write in order to know; write so that the reader may know.

Truth, Lies, and The Writer as Pretzel Baker

As the saying goes, there are lies, damned lies, and statistics. There are also literary lies. These are the good ones. Emily Dickinson is oft-quoted as writing, "Tell all the Truth but tell it slant." Almost a century later, the writers of *I Love Lucy* put a new twist on this concept when Ricky critiques Lucy's novel in progress:

> **Ricky:** But honey, it isn't true!
> **Lucy:** Ricky, that's what writers do, they take
> the truth and twist it a little.

(audience laughs)

> **Fred:** Well, if your book doesn't sell, you can
> always get a job making pretzels!

(big yuks)

When you write fiction or poetry directly from memory, the skill is partly in what you select to tell and how you order the material. Differentiate between the experience you had and the experience the poem or story will have. Even if they are consistent, they will likely not be congruent, as you select from, reshape, and re-proportion the material.

Like a sculptor, the writer chisels away what was in the experience that isn't in the story. Be careful not to take out essentials, throwing out the baby with the bathwater. (If you are writing about a baby taking a bath, don't throw out the bathwater.)

Some writers are blessed with great memories. Thomas Wolfe

could remember watching his sister climb a hill on her way to school when he was 18 months old, and he put that memory into *Look Homeward, Angel*. Also in *Angel*, he describes "the old cream-colored bed, painted gaily at head and foot with round medals of clustering fruit" in the boarding house based on the one his family ran in Asheville, where he hadn't been recently. I saw that bed. Sure enough, "round medals of clustering fruit" are painted gaily on it.

A flawed memory is not a fatal flaw; sometimes it can be an advantage. Filling a memory gap with invented truth may produce something more interesting—and appropriate to the story—than the actual experience. William Maxwell writes in his autobiographical short story "Billie Dyer": "For things that are not known—at least not anymore—and that there is now no way of finding out about, one has to fall back on imagination. This is not the same thing as the truth, but neither is it necessarily a falsehood." Even when attempting a faithful rendering of the past, we fall prey to imprecision. You can tell the truth about all you remember, but all you remember may not be the truth. In his preface to *Reveries Over Childhood and Youth*, W.B. Yeats writes: "I have changed nothing to my knowledge, and yet it must be that I have changed many things without my knowledge."

Here is an example of a tiny non-truth-non-falsehood. For a brief time, one of my neighbors was the novelist Davis Grubb (*Night of the Hunter, Fools Parade*). Years later, I wrote about the time I came across Davis in the hallway and asked him how his new novel was going. He replied, with exasperation, "I don't know, I don't know what's going to happen next," adding that he thought there might be a part in the movie for Jane Fonda. I also, in the piece, mentioned that he had a small dog named Howdy Rowdy whom he took by taxi to West Virginia, a nice little detail. Still more years later, I came across a photograph of Davis Grubb and his dog, taken around the time we lived in the same building. The dog's name: Rowdy Charlie. And, a friend is pretty sure that *he* told me Davis's comment about Jane Fonda.

Even if you do have a firm grasp on the truth of your memories, don't tell too much of it. Witnesses at a trial promise to tell "the truth, the whole truth, and nothing but the truth," but in literature the whole truth is usually more than we need. As Aristotle says, "History tells everything that happened within a period; drama is selective." Be careful not to overload the reader with too much drama-obscuring history. In *Take the Money and Run*, a witness is asked to recount the events that led to Woody Allen's character being apprehended. He starts to give a history of his day and gets hung up on what kind of juice he had that morning. Of course, Allen plays this for humor, but I have read some history-laden pieces that weren't so funny.

A side note: Writers usually must declare prose to be fiction or nonfiction, with all the respective freedom and responsibility. We don't do that with poetry. Magazines don't have sections for "fiction poetry" or "nonfiction poetry"; publishers don't label collections one way or the other; and writing programs don't offer two kinds of poetry workshops. Poets are free to vary their approach to the truth from line to line, poem to poem.

Invading Privacy

Virtually all books of fiction have a disclaimer stating that any resemblance to actual persons is coincidental, which should often be followed by a wink. Truth is, most writers frequently write about aspects of real people, and we may violate someone's privacy or reveal negative feelings and unflattering observations. Some writers find it relatively easy to assert their rights as sword-wielding artists protected by the shield of literature. Sherwood Anderson puts it bluntly: "If people did not want their stories told, it would be better for them to keep away from me." Other writers get queasy and hesitant, and let possible repercussions interfere with their writing.

Many feel that pain should only occur as an unavoidable by-product of the process, not as the goal of the product. David Ignatow cautions against using one's writing like a "sledgehammer on someone." I mentioned this to a writer known for his lack of inhibition in writing about people he knows, and he said, with the trace of a grin, "No, use it as a sledgehammer." It is a matter of personal choice; just don't be so naïve as to think that your writing will never affect anyone.

The good news is that often this is less of a problem than we might fear. A student wrote a story with a harshly depicted character based heavily on a friend, who admired the story and complimented, "My God, she's awful!" Dickens based his portrayal of Mrs. Nickleby on his mother, who didn't recognize herself. And to go from the sublime to the cartoonish: Legend has it that the voice of Daffy Duck was based on the quacky speech of a producer who, when asked his opinion of the voice, replied (sounding remarkably like Daffy Duck), "That's a funny voice! Where'd ya get that voice?"

When people do see themselves in a piece, they may be flattered, even proud at being portrayed. I used to write song lyrics, and one song was based on a falling-out with a friend. A couple of years later, he was sitting next to me in a club when the performer started the opening chords. I realized that I had never discussed the lyrics with my friend. He listened intently. When the song ended, before I could say anything, the waitress came over and my friend told her, smiling (I think more for my benefit), "Did you just hear that song? That was about *me!*" "Cool," the waitress said. *Cool*, I thought, but it was an odd sensation, sitting next to the real-life version of the character I had created out of words.

This phenomenon brings to mind these lines from Ezra Pound's "Canto II":

> *Hang it all, Robert Browning,*
> *there can be but the one "Sordello."*
> *But Sordello, and my Sordello?*

Pound is referring to three versions of Sordello: The 13th-century troubadour with that name; Browning's version of that person in his epic poem *Sordello* (which Pound once read out loud to Yeats at Stone Cottage); and Pound's own depiction of Sordello. Whenever you write about someone—even if you strive to be as faithful to the flesh and blood as possible—you create a *Sordello* of that person (if I may coin a phrase).

Sometimes we alter our portrayals in unflattering ways. Charles Dickens's wife's chiropodist, a dwarf, noticed herself in *David Copperfield*'s Miss Mowcher. She wrote an anguished letter to Dickens accusing him of linking Miss Mowcher's offensive traits to her "personal deformities." Dickens responded that his characters are composites, but he apologized for being the cause of such distress. The issue troubled him, and he wrote about the portrayal in a letter to someone else: "It is serio-comic, but there is no doubt one is wrong in being tempted to such a use of power."

This is an interesting case because the discussion occurred while *David Copperfield* was being serialized, and Dickens was receiving feedback before the work was finished. In a sense, all of London was his workshop. In later installments, Dickens fulfilled his promise to make Miss Mowcher a "very good character"— perhaps to the book's detriment. (The fact that Dickens also heard from the chiropodist's solicitor might have had something to do with Miss Mowcher's transformation.)

Sometimes the artistic problem is that we are *too* faithful to the real person or experience. We may be reluctant to graft fictionally appropriate traits onto a character who bears a non-coincidental resemblance to someone we know, or to invent details in a story that is predominately true. In these cases, you might need to adopt this attitude: *You're mine now. Who you are and what you do and think on these pages is up to me, and I will furnish the scenery however I please.* Nancy Hale's short story "Charlotte Russe" is based on dinner parties from her childhood. After reading the story, Hale's mother said, "That's the first I knew we had vast satiny napkins."

I suggest that you be bold in the writing but cautious in the sharing. If possible, discuss the process with the subject. If there are still issues, you may choose to limit consumption of the piece until the situation changes or you can figure out a way to make the writing more palatable without sacrificing quality. If you do bring such a piece to the workshop, you might ask for your copies to be returned, and perhaps remind your classmates of the need for confidentiality.

Let's consider another person who can be affected by your writing: *You.* Writers take a risk by exposing work that emanates from deeply felt experiences or revealing fantasies. A student commented, "I am not quite sure where my poems come from, and they appear, perhaps, a little stranger than I like to think I am." You will have to decide how much you are willing to reveal, but remember that in literature, strange can be good.

After I gave a reading of some delicate, personal work spiced with leaps into places I only knew in my imagination, someone remarked how brave I must be to "stand up there and say those things to strangers." I hadn't really thought about it, and I answered, "Well, it's me but it's not *me*." One of my *Sordello*s lived the experiences, another one showed up in the poems, and yet another performed them. Somehow—and this is the best part—I felt intact and pleased.

III

Notes on:
The Language

[A fisherman] asked me if I was using a sentipensante language, a feel-thinking language. And so, he was a master. I mean, I learned a lot from this sentence forever. I am a sentipensante.

— Eduardo Galeano

Prefatory Note: Conjurers

Magicians conjure with smoke and mirrors; writers make magic with words. Using language, Gabriel García Márquez not only conjures the village Macondo in *One Hundred Years of Solitude*, but he pulls gypsies out of his top hat and releases them to travel around town on a flying carpet.

Equally magical is the ability to make realistic images materialize. Poet Nick Bozanic describes the conjuring tasks he faced one morning: "What is the exact quality of light at 7 a.m. in late September, and 7 a.m. in early May? What is the difference between waking up in the morning when you're eight and when you're thirty-eight? How does it feel to be chained to a tree? How does it feel to catch a trout by the tail with your bare hands?"

I've heard a koan that presupposes a duck in a bottle and asks how to get the duck out without breaking the bottle. The answer (or so I've heard) is: "It's out." Now, it may take years of meditation to arrive at a true understanding of this, but my unenlightened guess is that it has something to do with the power of language.

In this section, I will explore how language can make such

magic as pulling rabbits out of hats and ducks out of bottles, while also capturing the light at 7 a.m. and the feel of a trout.

The Idea of Things

The poet Charles Reznikoff said in an interview: "You start with something that moves you and you state it as simply and as directly as possible, without saying you're moved, but in such a way that the reader will also be moved by it. This is the way I try to write." Reznikoff backed that up with an "ancient authority," quoting Wei T'ai, an 11th-century Chinese poet: "Poetry presents the thing in order to convey the feeling. It should be precise about the thing and reticent about the feeling."

Similarly, William Carlos Williams famously writes (in "A Sort of Song"): "No ideas / but in things." And perhaps the single most proffered advice in workshops is "Show, don't tell."

Yes, of course. But, also:

Exquisite, precise language can elevate ideas and feelings to the level of *things*. In 1938, at the age of 73, fifteen years after being awarded the Nobel Prize, William Butler Yeats ended his poem "Politics" with this couplet, which resonates even if you are not familiar with the preceding ten lines:

> *But O that I were young again*
> *And held her in my arms!*

No images, no similes, no details, no allusions, no gypsies on flying carpets, no ducks in or out of bottles. We don't *see* her or his arms. You don't have to look up any of the words or consult critical texts for obscure references. Countless writers before Yeats used each of those words, but Yeats was the first to put them in that particular order.

Take a minute and re-create what Yeats did: Write those lines longhand. Thirteen words, fourteen syllables. Simple? Yes. Simplistic (as in "unrealistically simple")? No.

If *simple* were easy, then everyone would do it. Running a marathon is simple; it's not easy.

The Elements of Voice

What is *voice*? The simple (simplistic?) answer: the words you choose and how you arrange them (just as one's fashion style consists of the selection and juxtaposition of clothing). Some writers' voices are distinctive primarily for their word choice, others for their sentence structure. Mostly, it's a combination of diction and syntax.

Do you have to achieve a distinctive voice, a way with words that tells the reader it is you (or a writer like you) behind the page? Not necessarily, but the reader should feel there is a *writer* behind the words. It is not as important for you to develop a consistent voice as it is for each piece you write to have a voice, which can change from piece to piece (just as your outfits vary depending on what or whom you are dressing for).

It is easier to experience voice than to describe it. In Harold Pinter's play *Betrayal*, Robert's wife admits that she has been having an affair with his best friend. Robert responds: "Ah. Yes. I thought it might be something like that, something along those lines." Try rewriting that response in a couple of other voices.

Listen to Thomas Pynchon's voice at the opening of *The Crying of Lot 49*: "One summer afternoon Mrs. Oedipa Maas came home from a Tupperware party whose hostess had put perhaps too much kirsch in the fondue to find that she, Oedipa, had been named executor, or she supposed executrix, of the estate of one Pierce Inverarity, a California real estate mogul who had once lost two million dollars in his spare time . . ." Now, listen as Pynchon departs 1960s California for colonial America in *Mason & Dixon*: "Snow-Balls have flown their Arcs, starr'd the Sides of Outbuildings, as of Cousins, carried Hats away into the brisk Wind off Delaware,— the Sleds are brought in and their Runners carefully dried and greased, shoes deposited in the back Hall, a stocking'd-foot Descent made upon the great Kitchen . . ."

Contrast Pynchon's voices with the opening of Ernest Hemingway's short story "The Battler": "Nick stood up. He was all right."

Writing voice can emanate from the ability to capture the music of colloquial speech. Boris Pasternak writes, "People discovered oratorical and melodic tendencies in my poems. This is not correct. They are there no more than in the speech of any ordinary person." Or, the writing can be composed on instruments that have been tuned differently from everyday speech, and the reader's ear needs to adjust. James Earl Jones writes about performing in August Wilson's *Fences*: "August was a poet before he became a playwright, and poetry is still part of the language his characters speak. You don't always hear people talk like that in real life, but you wish you could."

If your instrument makes quirky sounds, you might be developing a distinctive voice. But quirkiness does not always make for good writing; you might just be out of tune. That's why the ears of the workshop are so important.

Pegs and Holes

Writers spend a lot of time with pen poised in the air or fingers hovering over the keyboard, seeking out or waiting for the precise word. For an early draft, it may be best to settle for the roundest square peg at hand to go into the squarest round hole; otherwise, you may lose momentum. Later, you can look around for the right pegs or drill different holes.

Temporary words may wind up fitting after all. The lyrics for *Tea for Two* were originally intended as place-setters, but were never replaced. "Scrambled eggs, oh, my baby, how I love your legs" didn't fare as well in what became "Yesterday." (When Oscar Hammerstein was working on "Do Re Mi," how long did he search for a definition of *la* before he reconciled himself to "a note to follow *so*"?)

You don't even have to find a place-setter word—just leave an empty place. Ring Lardner claimed to *New Yorker* editor Herbert Ross that he followed this method to the extreme, writing "a few widely separated words or phrases on a piece of paper" and then going back to fill in the spaces.

As Compared to What?

In discussing André Breton's notions on surrealism, Anna Balakian writes that the value of a metaphorical image "consists not in an equivalence but in the subtraction of one set of associations from the other. The greater the disparity, the more powerful the light, just as in electricity the greater the difference in potential of the two live wires the greater the voltage."

Comparing Juliet with the sun doesn't mean she is ninety-three million miles away and you would be immolated if you went near her (though Romeo might have had a longer life if he had kept his distance).

Robertson Davies creates this electric simile in his novel *Fifth Business*: "My colleagues looked uncomprehendingly, like cows at a passing train." "

Colleagues compared to cows. Maximum voltage.

When I share this simile with students, I add: "Occasionally you may say something in the workshop that will evoke *cow looks* from your classmates." (Sometimes, the reaction I get after saying that makes me feel like a passing train.)

How Do You Truly Feel About Commas?

Punctuation marks guide the reader to avoid phrase collisions, and they affect the rhythmic aspect of the text's music. They can also have a dramatic impact on meaning. *My coworkers who like me are coming to my party* is different from *My coworkers, who like me, are coming to my party*. And, a million dollars (Canadian) was at stake in a contract dispute; Canada's telecommunications regulator, citing the "rules of punctuation," based his decision on the location of one comma in a fourteen-page document.

Many punctuation choices are determined by grammatical imperatives, but the author has some leeway, especially in poetry. I showed the fable writer Spenser Holst one of my poems. He asked me if I "loved" commas, adding, "If you do, use more of them in this poem. If you don't, take out the ones you have."

Depending on the piece—and the way you feel about commas, et al.—you can utilize *close* or *open* punctuation. An example of punctuation at its closest is this line from "The Betrothal" by Edna St. Vincent Millay, which has five commas in an eight syllable line: *Oh, come, my lad, or go, my lad*. If Millay had taken a wide open approach (*Oh come my lad or go my lad*), her meaning would not have been lost, but her music would have suffered. When a publisher added commas to A.E. Housman's lines starting with "Oh" (turning "Oh may I squire you round the meads" to "Oh, may I squire you round the meads"), Housman opted for a more open approach and deleted the commas.

Constructing a piece with open punctuation is like designing a road system with few signs and lights. It can be quite elegant, but you must be sure that the syntax controls the way the text is read; poets have the added resource of the line-break.

Accessorizing with Words

Reproduced images are constructed out of pixels, which our brains fill in and flesh out. (Look closely at an advertising poster.) Similarly, when we write, we build dialogue and description out of partial information. The difference is that a photograph will tend to look better with more information (although grainy can be artful), whereas a piece of writing can eventually collapse under the weight of its own language.

In *Amadeus*, the king tells Mozart that his new opera has too many notes. The same has been said to many writers, usually with more validity. Don't worry about using too many words while composing. For many writers, "more is more" in early drafts, and the final draft is likely to be shorter because contents tend to settle during revision.

The number of words optimal for any given piece depends on, well, the given piece. It was said about Joe DiMaggio that he could run as fast as he had to. Use as many words as you have to; any fewer and the piece doesn't reach its destination; any extra and you may overrun the meaning.

A student regularly wore about a dozen earrings to my workshop. She presented a particularly verbose poem, and I said, "This poem has so many great words that it doesn't need all those merely good words."

"And I don't need so many earrings," she replied. "But I *like* them."

"If you *love* the words, use them," was the best I could

counter, echoing what Spencer Holst had said to me, "but make sure it's true love. Use enough words to keep us fully in the piece, but not so many that we wish we were anywhere else."

One revision approach is to cut ruthlessly, then re-enter the words you feel bereft of. You may need to leave out fine material whose only fault is being in the wrong piece at the wrong time. It may be too much of a good thing, or a different kind of good thing.

A short story may be able to carry only so much weight outside the main story line, and a delicate poem might topple over with an extra image, just as in a dance an impressive somersault could derail a tender *pas de deux*. Count Basie advised trombonist Al Grey, "Don't try to play all you know in one night." I have taken trips on small airplanes where my suitcase wasn't at the baggage claim, not because it was lost but because the plane had reached its maximum weight and some luggage had to go on the next flight.

In a conversation with Martin Scorsese for *The New York Times Magazine*, Woody Allen stresses the importance of the will to delete: "But you could say universally *make it a little faster here* . . . That's one thing I think never hurts a film; I mean, if you can do it faster, do it. It's a godsend . . . Once you see it out, the joy of the speed is so exhilarating that I can never bring myself to put the material back."

Adjectives in particular undergo severe workshop scrutiny. We sometimes go overboard in our zealous disdain for these much maligned, often superfluous, sometimes merely ornamental words. The preceding sentence would have a different life without adjectives, as would the prose of Thomas Wolfe and Isaac Bashevis Singer, or this excerpt from the first sentence of William Faulkner's *Absalom, Absalom*: "From a little after two o'clock until almost sundown of the long still hot weary dead September afternoon they sat in what Miss Coldfield still called the office because her father had called it that—a dim hot airless room . . ."

Vicente Huidobro, in his poem "Ars Poetica," writes: "The adjective that bestows no life, destroys." Fair enough, but the other side of the coin is that the beneficent adjective bestows life.

As you revise, don't be automatically harsh on adjectives (and adverbs); try to determine if they are lifesavers or life-suckers. Throw the suckers overboard.

The Clarity of the Yellow Brick Road

An obsolete definition of *clarity* is "brilliancy, brightness, splendor, glory"—qualities we seek in our writing. A contemporary definition is "directness, orderliness, and precision of thought or expression." Anyone who has tried to assemble, say, an exercise bicycle has likely wished that the manual writer had workshopped the text for clarity. Literary writing that lacks clarity can engender similar frustration in the reader, and lucidity may be the single most important quality to consider as you revise.

Some writers hide behind obscurity. In the workshop, the more time spent deciphering, the less opportunity for critiquing. Some readers may even think that the harder it is to figure out a piece, the better it must be; or they may be reluctant to criticize what they don't understand. Former U.S. Poet Laureate Billy Collins told the online magazine *Guernica*: "I think clarity is the real risk in poetry because you are exposed. You're out in the open field. You're actually saying things that are comprehensible, and it's easy to criticize something you can understand."

This doesn't mean your work can't be difficult. Some responsibility must be borne by the reader, who may need to put on corrective lenses with a prescription tailored to the author's vision. William Carlos Williams puts it best in "January Morning": "I wanted to write a poem / that you would understand. / For what good is it to me / if you can't understand it? / But you got to try hard."

It is all right to expect a piece to be read more than once to get it *all*, but not to get it *at* all. In one of my workshops, the critique of a story got hung up on the setting. "It's some kind of a mental institution," said one student. "No, I think it's a resort hotel," said another. I did my workshop equivalent of Jimmy Durante's "Stop the music, stop the music" and asked the author, "Do you wish to enlighten us, so the critique doesn't go off the track?" The author replied that it was his dormitory. When I asked why he hadn't made that clear, he quoted a previous workshop teacher: "If I get one more story set in a college dorm, I'm going to scream."

I responded, "If I get one more story where an essential piece of information is willfully left out with no literary purpose, *I'm* going to scream." With the setting established, we were able to turn our attention to the metaphorical implications of the dorm's similarities with mental institutions and resort hotels.

Clarity in surrealistic writing is elusive but almost as important as in a depiction of a landscape or a narration of a meeting. A piece can be effective if your readers feel disoriented once inside, but we should not get lost trying to make our way *into* the piece; give us something to grasp. If I am driving through a disjointed, associative piece, I may not always know where I am or why, but I should have some confidence in the map provided by my travel agent, the writer. Even Dorothy has the clarity of the Yellow Brick Road.

Depth of field refers to the segment of a photographic image that is in sharpest focus. In a photograph with a small depth of field (such as many portraits) the background (or foreground) is intentionally blurry. With a large depth of field, the whole image may be sharp. Filmmakers sometimes shift focus from foreground to background, to redirect the viewer's attention without recomposing the frame.

When you write, if you make *everything* clear, the reader might become loaded down with details and not know what is important. A small depth of field is often effective. In the opening chapter of *Fathers and Sons*, Ivan Turgenev focuses on a strutting chicken being eyed with hostility by a cat, while blurring the shadowy entrance to the post-station in the background; the image of the chicken resonates.

A poem presented in one of my workshops was set in a playground. An interaction between two people received the same amount of clarity as the background. In this case, we agreed that the large depth of field worked because the piece wasn't about two people who happen to be in a playground; it was about a playground that happens to have two people in it.

Mysterious Capability

Mystery can be a key ingredient in making a piece wonderful, but mystery alone will not suffice. Hemingway, in *A Moveable Feast*, refers to paintings that he didn't like: "I did not understand them but they did not have any mystery." Authentic mystery can get the reader to care, while mystery for its own sake may not (unless you inadvertently tap into something significant in your unconscious, which is always possible).

John Keats, in an 1817 letter, defines *negative capability* as "when man is capable of being in uncertainties, Mysteries, doubts, without any irritable reaching after fact & reason." The key word is *irritable*—not all reaching for fact and reason generates irritability. Negative capability can be risky, betting all or nothing, but the writer and reader who can't live with it have much to live without.

Negative capability has been compared to Martin Heidegger's concept of *Gelassenheit*, which advocates "letting the Being of beings be." Every once in a while, as I am revising my work or critiquing someone else's, I come across something that I don't quite understand yet feel connected to, and I tell myself, "Let the Being of this being be."

License

Some creative writers think they have a 007 license to kill the language. The author shouldn't invoke *poetic license* (or, as they wrote in the 16th century, *lycence poetycall*) for every ungrammatical or illogical maneuver. You can't steer into ongoing traffic just because you have a driver's license.

The writer who diverts from the conventional has to build up trust with the reader, so the reader will be somewhat confident that a "mistake" or an oddity is on purpose and purposeful. As Bob Dylan sings, "To live outside the law you must be honest."

In his *Dream Songs*, John Berryman firmly establishes an unconventional voice, making "I'm scared a lonely" sound just right. And these lines from James Wright's "The Streets Grow Young" benefit from a cliché and an enallage (effective grammatical error): "Okay now, hit the road, and leave me / And my girl alone."

How much does our poetic license extend beyond language to content? How pliable to our words is the world around us?

Some people afford painters more leeway than writers to interpret (or defy) reality, but all artists should share the same freedom. Aristotle says, "The poet being an imitator, like a painter or any other artist, must of necessity imitate one of three objects—things as they were or are, things as they are said or thought to be, or things as they ought to be." Artists can interpret things as they appear *to them* by using distortion or hyperbole, as Pablo Picasso does in *Guernica* or Kafka in *The Trial.* The artist may also capture the way things *will* be: Picasso responded to complaints that Gertrude Stein did not look like his portrait of her by saying, "That does not make any difference, she will."

The artist's "fresh" take on something may actually help us see things as they are. In the early 1800s, John Constable dared to use shades of green when he painted landscapes; other English painters were using browns, based on the faded colors of the likes of Titian, and the Royal Academy's preference for ideal over natural landscapes. Constable's *Water Meadows Near Salisbury*—which now hangs in the Victoria and Albert Museum—was rejected by the Academy as a "nasty green thing." Constable responded to the notion that grass should be the hue of a Cremona violin by leading a committee to a meadow and placing a violin on the grass. Now, grass is green and Constable is one of the fathers of modern landscape painting.

Sometimes writers use their poetic license to cheat a bit about the way things are. George Venables ran into Wordsworth near Rydal "crooning out aloud some lines of a poem which he was composing." Wordsworth told Venables that he wanted "to make the shadow of Etna fall across Syracuse, the mountain being 40 miles from the city. Would this be possible?" Venables replied that the distance wasn't the problem; the "difficulty was that Etna is exactly North of Syracuse." To which Wordsworth implored that surely it is a little northeast or northwest. Venables let it go, realizing that Wordsworth was "determined to make the shadow fall the way he wanted it." And so we read in *The Prelude*: "Where Etna, over hill and valley, casts / His shadow stretching towards Syracuse."

No-Risk,
Risk-Taking Exercises

Prefatory Note

We learn to write by writing, so anything we write helps us learn to write. *Ergo*: Exercises help us learn to write.

When you are not expected to produce a polished, cohesive piece, you may let down your critical guard and take risks by treading unfamiliar or foreboding territory in form and language. I ask students not to discard their exercises, and it is not unusual for me to discover some of a student's strongest writing embedded in them. Many pieces reach the workshop table after starting out as exercises.

Even exercises that don't evolve keep you in writing shape. Baseball pitchers don't run when they pitch, but they run sprints in the outfield because they use their legs when they pitch. Exercises keep the writing legs strong (and increase stamina).

Most of these exercises can be done repeatedly. Ignore or modify any or all instructions that interfere with your creative flow. And, most importantly, relax and enjoy them.

Winter Counts

Tribes of the Sioux Nation (among other Plains Indians) maintained historical calendars comprised of *winter counts*. Tribe historians would depict a significant event for each year on a buffalo or deer skin. The story behind each pictograph would be passed along verbally, and several annotated winter counts survive.

Here are a few examples from The Big Missouri Winter Count, which runs from 1796 to 1926.

> **1808:** Indians expressed gratitude to Providence in profuse manner by putting many red flags on hills, rocks, and other conspicuous places.

> **1824:** The winter was so severe that the Sioux camped near a fine field of corn raised by a whiteman. He gave them corn to eat.

> **1834:** The winter the stars fell.

> **1905:** The wife of Leader Charge gave birth to quadruplets.

> **1918:** Many young men joined the Army to fight in World War I.

Barry Holstun Lopez intersperses winter counts throughout the title story of his collection *Winter Count*, including:

> **1809:** Blue feathers found on the ground from unknown birds.

> **1847:** One man alone defended the Hat in a fight with the Crow.

> **1875:** White Hair, he was killed in a river by an Omaha man.

For this exercise, divide your age into five segments (if you are 25, it would be birth–5, 5–10, 10–15, 15–20, 20–25). Write a "winter count" for each segment: an image, a momentous event, or something seemingly insignificant that has risen to the surface. Keep them short (no more than a few sentences each).

Flesh out any that intrigue you, and put the others into storage.

Maintain a contemporary winter count, with at least several entries a week.

Silent Film

Write a prose narrative for a short film (three minutes or less) with no dialogue. Write it so that the camera operator could film directly from your story; everything should be visual and external. There are no limits on budget. The film can be realistic or surrealistic. It can have a narrative or associative structure. Use the present tense.

Righteous Plagiarism

In his *Paris Diary*, Ned Rorem makes an interesting point about plagiarism: "It is a *conscious plagiarism* that demonstrates invention: we are so taken with what someone else did that we set out to do likewise. Yet prospects of shameful exposure are such that we disguise to a point of opposition; then the song becomes ours. No one suspects. It's *unconscious* stealing that's dangerous."

Select a piece of writing you admire, and consciously plagiarize it. The catch is that you have to demonstrate invention and make it become yours.

Be a Flâneur

Designate an hour to be a flâneur (think: window shopping with your entire surroundings as your window), in the tradition of Baudelaire and extolled by Walter Benjamin, who defines it as "botanizing on the asphalt." Pick a starting point (anywhere in your town where you feel safe), and then *stroll* rather than *walk*. Balzac may overstate it when he says, "To walk is to vegetate, to stroll is to live," but you catch the distinction. Don't plan your route. Look, listen, take notes. Give everything a fair chance for your attention: the tops of buildings, storefronts, people, animals. Observe interactions but stay apart. The title of your piece could be the location and time of your stroll.

As a variation, repeat at the same location but at a different time (the main business street during a workday morning and a weekend evening).

Literary Stalking

While on a bus or subway, in a café or on the street, select a person you don't know who interests you in some way. "Sketch" a portrait of that person in words: clothes, expression, stance, gait, etc. Be discreet. Later, with your imagination, "follow" the person somewhere and change his or her life, in a large or tiny but meaningful way.

Personal Effects

The term *personal effects* can refer to items a traveler brings "for use and comfort" or to possessions distributed to beneficiaries. Herbert Read writes, "Nothing is so expressive of a man as the fetishes he gathers round him—his pipe, his pens, his pocket knife—even the pattern of his suit." Tim O'Brien's powerful short story "The Things They Carried" contains lists of objects—required and elective—carried by American soldiers in Vietnam, including: P-38 can openers, heat tabs, mosquito repellent, chewing gum, candy, packets of Kool-Aid, lighters, sewing kits, a diary, an illustrated New Testament, comic books, dental floss.

Create two or three characters and make annotated lists of their personal effects (what the items look like, where they came from, etc.). Then, write a story with these characters, using as many of the items as possible.

Punctuation

Select a paragraph or two by someone who writes complex sentences (Henry James, Marcel Proust, William Faulkner). Read the excerpt a few times, focusing on the punctuation. Feel the rhythmic flow without paying much attention to the content, as if you were concentrating on the percussion channel of a jazz recording. Appreciate the commas and semicolons, just as you would drums and bass.

Copy just the punctuation. Insert your own words (any number you wish) between the marks.

Next, "write" a piece consisting exclusively of punctuation marks, lots of them, all kinds. Then add words.

Plucking Words

A simple loosening-up exercise. Open any book you have around. Pick an interesting word from the left page and one from the right page. Open another book and do the same. Write three or four paragraphs, each one containing all four words. (Here are four words I just plucked: *polite, complaint, tower, mystery.*)

Expand/Contract

Write a piece of any nature, approximately fifty words.

Expand it to about one hundred words, adding text anywhere: You can flesh out existing sentences, start the piece earlier, end it later, and/or follow any leads in between.

Contract it back to fifty (by whatever means you wish).

Repeat.

Keep repeating until the fun stops.

The Ultimate Unreliable Narrator

Write a brief lecture about something you know little or nothing about. Don't do research. You may misuse words but don't make up any. Some examples: computer chip manufacturing, brain surgery, a dialogue between Freud and Picasso, building the New York City subway system, Einstein's secret diary, your parents' first date.

The News

1. In Thomas Wolfe's *You Can't Go Home Again*, the narrator

quotes a short newspaper article: "An unidentified man fell or jumped yesterday at noon from the twelfth story of the Admiral Francis Drake Hotel . . ." For the next fifteen pages, Wolfe invents the story behind this tragic tidbit, concluding with: "That was the news. Now you've had the story."

Scour the newspaper for similarly intriguing but incomplete news, and make up the story. (Here's one from the archives: "Michigan's homemaker of the year was bound over for trial in Shiawassee County Circuit Court on a murder charge . . . [She] is charged with shooting to death her husband . . . as he lay in bed in their Owosso home on November 15.")

2. Reading *The New York Times*, I was taken by a feature about tough times in a small town. A 50-year-old man had returned home to live with his mother and was hoping to get a job at the new Wal-Mart. "The wheel goes round. Sonny Boy came home," he said.

That quote kept running through my mind, and I asked my current workshop to write a piece incorporating "Sonny boy came home." For the remainder of the term, the phrase occasionally turned up in stories we were critiquing, always coming as a surprise, each story different from the other.

Extract a compelling quote or phrase from a newspaper or magazine article and write a piece around it—in a totally different context.

Chord Changes

Think of words as having the same relationship to an image as musical notes have to a chord. Adding or changing one note in a chord can affect the mood of the sound (major to major seventh, or minor to major).

Create a series of unrelated phrases, then alter the mood of each by changing or adding one or more words. For example: "a child prancing with a balloon" could become "a child with a pin prancing with a balloon" or "a child weeping with a balloon."

Time Bomb

Establish a character and set an emotional time bomb to go off in sixty minutes: an "explosion" of love, salvation, despair, or simply exuberance at being alive. Write the events—internal and external—of the sixty minutes that lead to the explosion. Tick, tick, tick.

I'm Trying

In a small group discussion, I asked the writer Peter Marin a difficult question; he paused, frowning, and responded deliberately, "I don't know, but I'm trying to write about it." That was a *writer* talking, and I was more impressed than if he had already written about it and poured out a bottled answer. (I love the sound of "I'm trying to write about it." It can be a convenient answer to many questions, from "How are you?" to "What's *Finnegans Wake* all about?")

Make a list poem (perhaps in a notebook) with each line starting "I'm trying to write about . . ." ("I'm trying to write about Paris in the snow," "I'm trying to write about my grandmother.") Refer to this list from time to time until you have tried to write about everything on it. Start a new list.

Review

Alastair Reid writes of Borges: "He told me once that as a young man he had contemplated writing a long dynastic novel encompassing the history of Argentina since independence, until he realized that he could write, in the span of a few pages, a descriptive review of just such a work by an invented author, adding his reflections on the genre." Borges did go on to invent authors, among them Mir Bahadur Ali (and review his equally nonexistent book *The Approach to Al-Mu'tasim*).

Invent an author (including a biographical note for the book jacket), and make up a critic (also with a biographical note). Write the critic's review of the author's book.

Then, write an exchange of cranky letters between the author and the critic (the kind that enliven the pages of such publications as the *The New York Times Book Review*).

Three Stories

Write a short story comprised of three sentences of any length (a beginning, a middle, and an end). Then write two additional three-sentence stories. The first sentence of story #2 should be an associative leap from the last sentence of #1, and the first sentence of story #3 should be an associative leap from the last sentence of story #2. (This is based on *renga*, a Japanese poetry form.)

Layering

Compose by layering words like paint. First tell the bare bones of a story, as sparsely as possible. In each succeeding draft, add a layer (dialogue, setting, images, omniscient narrator's interjections, exposition, etc.). Put each layer in a different typeface. See what happens if you separate the layers and present the story with the layers *following* one another, rather than being integrated into the narrative.

Make Me Laugh

Write something so over-the-top bad that your workshop would be tempted to respond with derisive laughter. (It's not so easy.)

Guidelines

I once considered writing a romance novel to help support my literary writing. I obtained the guidelines for a particular series, which included four pages of caveats, such as: "Her first relationship must have been serious enough for her to have felt she was in love and committed, and it must have ended before the start of the novel." "The hero ('Mr. Right'—the second love) is introduced in the first chapter." "Despite the conflicts and complications between the heroine and hero, the story is upbeat in tone." "The hero and heroine do make love even when unmarried, and with plenty of sensuous description. But the explicit details will be used only in foreplay." "Limit—severely—the use of flashback."

I wound up declining, not because it was beneath me as an artist but because it seemed too hard.

But I got the idea for a group exercise: Collectively decide on guidelines for a short story, essay, or poem. Make them as complicated and/or silly as you wish. Then, each of you write a piece following the guidelines. One of the requirements should be length, and you might want to keep it short (e.g., two-page prose pieces, eighteen-line poems). Collect them into a booklet.

Leave a Poem

This is more an exercise in distribution than composition. In the 8th century, Li Po cast poems into the river. Write a poem— or anything else—and leave it to be discovered. You can leave it for a specific person (in a place where you know he or she will find it) or deposit it where anyone might come across it (you'll never know). Unlike Li Po, you should make a copy of the poem before you cast it off. (Li Po tended to go a bit overboard: legend is he died trying to embrace the moon—in a river.)

End of Season Piece

At the end of the day, several generations ago, some foun-tain pen makers combined the leftover celluloid or plastic and swirled it together to create "end-of-day" pens, which might make little overall sense but certainly have their moments. (This was also done by manufacturers of other types of plastic and glass products.)

At the end of each season, gather your leftovers and frag-ments from poems, stories, shopping lists, letters, etc. and blend them into an end-of-season piece. Continuity (of any sort) is optional.

To prepare for this exercise, you must not throw anything out. Every time you cut from a piece or abandon a piece alto-gether, store the material in your end-of-season folder.

Prepping for the Workshop

(a.k.a. Notes on: Revision)

Prefatory Note

The following suggestions can help you examine your classmates' writing in preparation for the critique, and they can also be useful as you revise your own work.

I suggest that you make copies of your classmates' pieces before you start working on them: You'll have a work copy to scrawl on, and a clean copy to mark up for the author when you know exactly what you want to say.

Don't use this section as a checklist for critique or revision; the process should not be that methodical. Let the pieces breathe. Strategies like these work best when we internalize them, when we let what we know help govern what we do, without necessarily making the connection at the time.

These notes are in no particular order, except for the first and the last.

Get Inside

Get "inside" the piece, which usually takes a couple of readings.

Reach a comfort level where you feel like you could talk about the piece to someone who hasn't read it, and you have a sense of what needs to be accomplished for it to succeed. If you can't get inside a piece, put it aside for a while and take a fresh look at it. Sometimes it's amazing how much a piece can change without anyone touching it.

Who's Talking and When?

Look closely at the point of view and verb tenses. Did the author make the best choices to tell the story? Might a first-person piece be more effective in the third person? Past tense better than present tense? How many heads—if any—should the author get into for a third-person piece? Are there any un-warranted deviations from the established point of view? If so, would you suggest fixing them, or changing the point of view? Likewise with tenses.

LCG (Linguistic Cardiogram)

Imagine hooking up a "linguistic-cardiogram" to the piece. Where does it get excited? Where does it skip a beat? Where does it go "code blue"? Where does it revive? Indicate such places on the manuscript. Even if you do not have specific comments, you might have occasion to point to them.

In and Out

What phrases or sentences take you inside the piece? Where do you think: *I'm sold, let me see what else you have for me to buy?*

What phrases or sentences take you out of the piece, perhaps because they trip you up syntactically or seem implausible? Are there any pinpricking lines that cause the air to fizzle out? Are there any detailed scenes where a short summary might suffice? Summaries that should be stretched out?

Questions

What's at stake–what can be lost or gained? What would readers be deprived of if this piece did not exist or was not understood? If you can't find anything, can you suggest how the stakes might be raised?

Who are these people? Why are we reading about them? What happens *to* them? What do they *make* happen?

Where are the roadblocks? What happens on the detours?

What are the most amazing *plausible* possibilities?

What if?

Ask yourself, "What else do I want to know?" Ask the author, "Do you want to tell us?"

Research Possibilities

Could the piece benefit from research? One of my students wrote a story in which a lizard "hissed." Another student wondered whether lizards actually hiss, and no one in the room knew for sure, including the author. I suggested that she do some research on lizards; she would find the answer and might discover something else about lizards. (Yes, many lizards do hiss when threatened, and they also thrash their tails.)

Research does not have to involve books and databases. I wrote a short story called "Playing Piano at my Ex-Fiancée's Wedding" and showed it to the poet and editor Bill Zavatsky. In one scene, the band eats leftovers after the affair, as the bride and groom are leaving. Zavatsky (a self-described "old gig musician") responded that the band is never served leftovers, and they dine when the guests do or shortly after. He also mentioned that he had "never played or attended a wedding where the bride and groom stayed to the end." My revised eating scene takes place at a better point in the story, and once I got the bride and groom out of there I was able to write a scene—which the story sorely needed—between the narrator (who is in disguise) and the bride's mother.

Story and Plot

Loosely speaking, *story* can be thought of as a narrative involving one or more characters, and *plot* as the selection, sequencing, and length of scenes used to tell the story. Are there problems with the story or with the plot? If you summarized the story to someone, would it sound better than it actually reads? Or would it read better than it sounds?

A student was aware that her short story wasn't working, but she wasn't sure how to approach it. She asked another student to explicate the story, and when he was able to do it to her satisfaction, she recorded the good news in her notebook: "He grasped the *story*; he found the narrative *whole*, albeit deficient structurally." Confident that her story was sound, she was able to focus on the language and how to manipulate the sequence of scenes.

Mistaken Identity

Is the piece in the wrong genre? This gets tricky if you are in a single-genre workshop (where it would be out of bounds to change a story into a poem), but such a suggestion can be pivotal in a multi-genre workshop. I suggested that a student change a personal essay into fiction, and the student felt released from fidelity to the facts, yet more able to confront the truth. "What a change it makes when you call it another thing!" she said.

Locate the Tongue

Are there places where you're not sure if the author's (or a character's) tongue is pressed inside the cheek? Not knowing whether something is ironic or straightforward, serious or satirical, can cause a story, essay, or poem to be misread. But satire can be less effective if it is *too* obvious. I wouldn't have suggested that Jonathan Swift move his tongue in "A Modest Proposal," even though many thought he was seriously advocating cannibalism as a response to poverty. You can help the author place the tongue in the optimal location for the piece by inserting an irony-detecting laser into the author's mouth and gently using tongs to move the tongue to the appropriate spot.

Turns

Sometimes we write our way into a corner and can't get out; other times we write our way into a stadium and the reader can't find us. Look for any wrong turns the author may have made that led to such predicaments.

Top and Bottom

Take especially close looks at beginnings and endings. Does the story or poem start or end too soon or too late? Does it reach the optimal amount of closure? Has anything been promised to the reader that hasn't been delivered? Has anything been delivered that wasn't paid for?

Movement

Some pieces need to move as directly as a cab ride (should), while others are out for a Sunday drive. Determine what governs the movement through the piece (chronology, association, memory, thematic connections), and see if anything breaks that flow without just cause. Do any flashbacks seem like they are making up for something the author neglected to tell, perhaps because the author just realized it had to have happened? If so, where might such scenes be placed in the narrative? Is the piece optimally broken into paragraphs (or stanzas), sections, chapters, and parts? A piece of writing doesn't need to move seamlessly, but the seams should be as functional and beautiful as those on a baseball.

What's in a Title?

Does the piece need to have a more effective title, perhaps providing some vital information the reader should know going in, or previewing a crucial detail or image? Some titles are merely "names," providing us with something to call the piece but not offering much else—and that's all they need to be.

Sticking Together

A poem or story doesn't necessarily have to be coherent (logically or aesthetically consistent), but it should be cohesive (sticking together) in some way. Is there any place the piece becomes unglued? Look for setups that have no payoffs, and payoffs that have no setups. Look for inconsistencies; authors can break lots of rules but should pay attention to the ones *they* set for a given piece.

Changes

Examine how, why, and when characters change. *Change* is not a required element for a poem, but is expected in a short story or novel (a point driven home to me when I showed one of my first stories to Dwight Macdonald, who responded that the writing was fine but "nobody changes").

Are changes gradual or abrupt? Does a character crack up or get progressively flaky until bonkers; does someone snap with anger or do a slow burn, moving inexorably toward a tantrum; do two people fall madly in love or creep from friendship to romance? Are there appropriate precipitating circumstances for these changes? If a straw is going to break a camel's back, there have to be many previous straws, or it has to be one hell of a straw.

Hide and Seek

You may have to search to find the poem or story hidden in the draft. T. S. Eliot gave Ezra Pound "the manuscript of a scrawling, chaotic poem," and Pound suggested wholesale deletions. *The Waste Land* (and Eliot's career) was better for it. If you feel such drastic cutting is appropriate, make sure the author takes it as the compliment it is.

Or, you may detect the makings of more than one poem or story within a submission, a situation that should likewise make the author feel fortunate.

Revision as Evolution

The parts of an evolving organism tend to become more complex as modifications improve form and function. A piece of writing progressing through drafts can become similarly differentiated, as the author fleshes out the text. But, just as fitness in nature can be enhanced through winnowing (snakes "lost" their legs), text can be improved by simplifying—a kind of internal "survival of the fittest." Picasso's depictions of a bull in his 1945 series of lithographs evolve through such simplification. (The lithograph pressman commented, "And I couldn't help thinking to myself: What I don't understand is that he has ended up where he ought to have begun!")

Some writers find it more beneficial to write complex first drafts and simplify, while others keep building. Look for ways the piece might evolve in either direction.

Problems and Opportunities

Whenever you discover a problem in a piece, one response might be to blot it out, achieving addition by subtraction. But many problems are also opportunities. If a character's action is unmotivated, perhaps an earlier scene or detail could be added or modified to make it work. If a scene appears to be unrealistic, maybe it could be turned into a dream or fantasy.

Tell, Don't Show

No, this isn't a typo. Look for places where the author showed what might have been told. I've read stories in which the writer was so afraid of committing a *show-don't-tell* violation that the narrative got bogged down in "show business." That's not natural storytelling. A student once asked me to point out "places where I can tell instead of show," as if looking for dispensation. I was glad to oblige.

Technicalities

Copyediting is not part of your job description in preparing for a critique, but watch for technical missteps that could have particularly deleterious effects, such as problems with antecedents. *He, she, it,* and *they* should not require you to get on your hands and knees to find whom they belong to, and a misreading can have nasty consequences.

Applause, Applause

Pick sentences or images to savor and applaud. Let the author know when something has delighted or touched you, has made you laugh or cry, or has elicited jealousy ("I wish I had written that"). Laud them during the critique or mark them on the manuscript.

Are You Convinced?

Ultimately, what really matters is if the piece is convincing. If you are convinced, then it may be best not to dwell on any of the above.

PART TWO

Notes on Workshopping

I

Notes on:

The Workshop

I felt like I belonged somewhere.

– Anne Sexton, speaking about her
workshop with Robert Lowell
at Boston University

Prefatory Note: A Way of Being in the World

We often hear writers talk about their fear of the empty page—one could scare guests at a literary Halloween party by wearing a blank sheet—but we hear less about how frightening the *full* page can be: *What do I do now?*

That's when the workshop can enter the picture. The image of writing as a lonely endeavor—private struggles leading to emergences with finished products—holds true for some lone-wolf writers. Others travel in packs consisting of editors, agents, friends, relatives, and fellow writers. A workshop provides you with an instant pack. (After you have had your fill of workshops, it may be time to howl on your own for a while.)

Being in a workshop empowers you. You not only have the right to write, you have the obligation. When I was a newspaper reporter, I felt entitled to speak to anyone about anything; indeed, I would be negligent *not* to speak to someone vital to my story, whether out of shyness, laziness, or fear. The workshop can provide you with the needed boost to speak to yourself and invite others to overhear.

When you enroll in a workshop you render irrelevant the

question "Am I worthy of writing?" You *must* do it, just as in a physics class you must strive to understand *force to the fulcrum*.

In his poem "The Camp," Hayden Carruth calls writing a "way of being in the world." In the workshop you have others to *be* with. The likes of Emily Dickinson did quite well in isolation, but most of us need readers to help us become better writers. In "The Death of the Hired Hand," Robert Frost defines *home* as the place where "they have to take you in." The workshop is the place where they have to read you. And being in a workshop requires us to read ourselves, very carefully.

"I need a little honest help," Thomas Wolfe wrote to his editor, Maxwell Perkins. A good workshop provides you with a roomful of honest help. But how do we define *honesty* in this context? You can honestly say that you hate a story, but only someone capable of being fueled by revenge will become a better writer from hearing it. The workshop requires that everyone do an *honest day's work*, thoroughly reading and considering one another's submissions, and make a good-faith effort to be helpful. In one of my first workshops, I received this gem: "This just doesn't make me *feel* anything." Honest? I assume so. Helpful? Decidedly not.

History in a Paragraph

The University of Iowa offered its first creative writing course in 1897. By the 1920s, Columbia University had a full-scale program, including poetry, fiction, and "photoplay" writing. The term *writers' workshop* was first used officially at the University of Iowa in 1939; another innovation that year was a course in six-man football. Now there are hundreds of graduate and undergraduate writing workshop programs and thousands more workshops in community centers, libraries, and living rooms (whereas the six-man football movement seems to have petered out). The creative writing workshop remains largely an American notion; in the classrooms of other countries, for the most part, one *studies*—rather than *makes*—literature, and writing classes focus on composition or criticism. This is changing, with workshop programs now prevalent in such countries as England and Australia. (The Australian Association of Writing Programs publishes an excellent online journal, *Text*.)

Working at the Shop

The workshop is where part of the writing work gets done, not displayed. It is a studio, not a gallery. You come to the workshop to improve the work, not to perform and be judged. You do not solicit—nor offer—book reviews. No single critique (or entire workshop term) should lead to the determination "This is how good I am and will ever be."

Writing is a process of discovery, and your understanding of what you discover in solitude can be deepened by hearing thoughtful people comment on your work. Workshopping becomes part of your writing process, as you invite shopmates to join you in considering further revision. You are the writer of first resort and the editor of last resort. Each piece you take to the workshop will have many suitors with ideas about its future prospects, but it will go home with you.

A student of mine wrote first drafts in a school notebook that had spaces on the cover for "Subject" and "Professor." The student had written "Creative Writing" for the subject and "Me" for the professor.

By All, For All

The work is done by all, for all. One must always be vigilant, no matter whose piece is being discussed. To illustrate (in a roundabout way): I was in the dentist's chair with the assistant's finger in my mouth. The dentist said, "Bite down," and I did. Right on her finger. The dentist said to his assistant, "When I tell him to bite down, you need to take your finger out." Three lessons here, applicable to the workshop:

1. You must pay attention to everything, even if you are not being directly addressed, because you never know what might affect you.

2. Unlike what I did, consider the implications of what someone says before you act on it.

3. Someone can get hurt.

As long as I'm in the dentist's office, here's another true parable. I used to have a dentist who made me feel guilty for being in the very condition that I was paying him to deal with. I went to a new dentist and sheepishly opened my mouth. He smiled and said, "You *need* me!"
Two lessons here:

1. Don't get annoyed at writing you feel is deficient. Your attitude should be: "You need me!"

2. Don't be hesitant to bring in a piece that you know has problems. Open wide.

In a typical workshop, you may have a piece on the table for critique three or four times per term. This does not mean that you perform community service for your classmates on the weeks you are not "up." You don't *give* in order to earn your chance to *get*. We learn by being intimately involved with other people's writing over a stretch of time: choice of subject matter, structural and linguistic decisions, how pieces evolve through revision.

We all know the value of learning from our mistakes; in the workshop, we can learn from others' "mistakes," and also from their successes. A student brought in a story in which two characters walk and talk along the Washington Mall. The narrative was all walk and talk and no conflict, no sizzle. At the end of the critique, the author lamented that she had no idea how to accomplish what we were suggesting. A few weeks later, during a discussion of someone else's piece—one with sizzle—she turned to me and whispered, "Now I get it."

How the Workshop Works

The aim of the workshop is to move the writing along, mostly by means of group critiques. Time may also be devoted to: discussing the work of published writers, presenting writing assignments (perhaps to be done in-class), talking about craft issues, and, occasionally, whining and commiserating.

Here is a template for the critique, with variations.

Drafts of pieces (which might be in response to an assignment) are distributed in advance (either hard copy or email). If pieces are not handed out in advance, the critique is preceded by an out-loud reading (usually by the author, but sometimes by the teacher or another student). Otherwise, the reading might be waived, especially for longer pieces (although the teacher may ask to hear a brief excerpt).

Instructors usually do not permit the author to preface the critique with caveats, apologies, or explanations. Many writers are prone to prolepses (stating or responding to an objection before it is made), which are likely to taint their classmates' reactions. If you do have the opportunity to make a comment before a piece is read or discussed, avoid belittling your own work ("This is really terrible" or "I just tossed this off at 3 a.m."). Your intention may be to inoculate yourself from criticism, but your classmates could wonder why they should be expected to care more than you seem to.

The teacher starts with brief comments or questions to frame the critique, or throws it open to the class. I occasionally begin by asking everyone to say something, anything, about the piece, but keep it to a sentence or two. They could mention a problem area (especially any clarity issues that could hamper the discussion) or a phrase they like; they might simply describe an aspect of the piece ("It's a first-person story taking place over one afternoon"; "It has many images"). After going around the table (or halfway if it's a big group), we usually have a pretty good sense of how to approach the work, and we've gotten everyone's voice out there early.

The teacher conducts the discussion. Your teacher may resemble an orchestra conductor, wielding his or her "call-on" nod like a baton: "hushing" a topic (*pianissimo*) or encouraging it to be discussed more vigorously (*forte*). If the piece is short and class-time is long, the teacher may conduct a more leisurely critique (*adagio*); with the session coming to an end and much to talk about, the teacher may pick up the pace (*allegro*).

Discussing what is positive about a piece—before taking on what isn't working—can enhance the author's equilibrium so that he or she will not be thrown off balance when hearing what might be lacking. However, this can backfire if it is done by rote ("first the good news, then the bad news"). Authors might feel like they are being set up for the blows they know will come, and perhaps even find it hard to accept the sincerity of the positive comments. (In fact, we shouldn't get too hung up on classifying comments as *positive* or *negative*; all comments should strive to be *helpful*.)

The teacher's role can range from moderator to dominator. Some teachers intersperse their comments throughout the conversation. Others wait until the students have finished before weighing in; during the body of the discussion they focus on asking questions and keeping the critique on track.

Most teachers ask the author to maintain a vow of silence until the last part of the critique (and some might ask the author not to talk even then). It is difficult to listen and take notes while engaging in a discussion about your own work. And a peremptory response deprives you of discovering what others think. For example, someone says, "I think Susan is being sarcastic when she tells John his shoes are cool," and the author jumps in with: "No, she really likes them." Better to hear how the others view Susan's comment. If respondents ask questions (such as "What that real or a dream?" or "Why does she throw a drink in his face?"), the author should let others answer.

One student objected to such restraints by protesting that she was being deprived of her freedom of speech. I responded, "You are also being deprived of your right to bear arms in class. Actually, I am only *delaying* your freedom of speech." Some students have gotten around the no-speaking rule by shaking their head *yes* or *no*. Communication doesn't require phonation: just ask Marcel Marceau or Bill Irwin, and watch for the response.

That said, I have become somewhat flexible in letting the author speak during the critique in specific instances and under supervision. While it is true that you won't be able to accompany your piece to readers beyond the workshop, the draft on the table is *not* the version that will be out there. I ask authors to use restraint, but they may raise their hand (subtly) if absolutely compelled. I'll usually ask the nature of their comment; most can wait until the end of the critique.

If a critique gets stuck on a specific point, I may interrupt the proceedings and appeal for a ruling from the author. Once, while discussing a story, we got bogged down in the relationship between a male and female sitting on a couch. We had gone far enough for us to agree that the relationship was both crucial and unclear. I said to the author, "Okay, you should note that this is an issue to be dealt with. For the sake of the critique, could you clarify it for us?" (They were brother and sister, not lovers as some had thought.)

When discussing a first-person piece, students sometimes assume that the narrator is the same gender as the author, which may not be the case. Also, confusion can be caused by the unstated gender of a singular *you* (which occurs often in poetry). In either instance, I may ask the author to clarify the gender for the purpose of the critique; an author may feel uncomfortable listening to, say, a discussion that misidentifies one or both genders in a piece about a romantic relationship. We may then consider whether the gender should be made explicit.

Near the end, the author is usually given the chance to ask questions and perhaps pursue issues raised by the discussion. This should be an opportunity to gather and clarify, not to rebut. If you debate the merits of some aspect of your story—rather than try to enhance your understanding of how the story is being received—you may win the argument but lose the story.

The teacher brings the critique to closure with a concluding statement or summary of points for the writer to contemplate.

The author goes home encouraged, energized, and armed with wonderful ideas for revision. The other students go home feeling good about themselves and the world and eager for their turn to be critiqued. The teacher goes home and writes paragraphs like this.

The Draft Critique

If you feel stifled by restrictions on authorial commentary during the workshop, you might want to organize informal *draft critiques* outside the classroom. In a draft critique, the author can speak with impunity, even lead the discussion. I stumbled upon this approach when a student showed up for class saying he was unprepared; he just couldn't get his story together, but he did have some fragments, notes, and ideas. We had some extra time, so we talked about his material, and the session proved to be quite helpful.

In a draft critique, your classmates are like guests who come early to the party to help put out the food and arrange the flowers. A draft critique can provide a well-timed boost, but don't let it close the door to self-discovery.

Nitpicking

A teacher may let the workshop dwell on something small, such as a comma or a word choice, because one punctuation mark or word can be pivotal. (John Masefield's "Sea-Fever" was first published with the opening line "I must go down to the seas again"; about twenty years later, Masefield changed it to "I must down to the seas again." After another twenty years, he "repented and put 'go' back.") These discussions also demonstrate how a group of intelligent people can get worked up over subtle points of language or punctuation. Nitpicking usually comes toward the end of the critique, when the larger issues have been aired, but sometimes the teacher might allow—or even encourage—a small item to be picked over earlier, to vary the pace of the discussion or to let larger issues marinate.

Some students apologetically preface comments with, "This

is nitpicking." *Nit* used to mean "to pore carefully over a book." In another context, *nitpicking* literally refers to "extricating lice." This may sound unappealing, but the mutual grooming practiced by many animal species has the dual effect of cleansing the recipients and fostering community.

So, pick that nit. Gently undangle that participle, extricate that irritating comma. The author will feel better and everyone will feel closer. As the narrator of George Moore's *A Mummer's Wife* says, "Anyone who can improve a sentence of mine by the omission of or placing of a comma is looked upon as my dearest friend."

Trusts and Bonds

During the first class of the term, look around the room. Over the next few months you will get to know these people in ways you probably would not in other classes. You will become acquainted with their pains, joys, and imaginings. You may learn things about them that their friends and family don't know.

While this may or may not turn out to be a legendary workshop to be remembered for years, you will almost certainly come to trust and respect one another, and wish you had felt that way earlier in the term. It is tempting to say, "Hey, we're going to wind up being a tight group and wish we had come together sooner, so why don't we start now?" But that would be like saying to a writer, "Why don't you skip the first five drafts and go right to the final one?"

One way to build trust is to critique the *piece*, not the *author*. Anne Sexton said about her workshop teacher Robert Lowell:

"If he was unkind to the poem, he was never unkind to the poet."

Some workshops—like some poems—click right away, and others take more time. Try to bond as quickly as naturally feasible. In a midterm evaluation, a student wrote: "It seems that *risk* should be a bigger factor in this class. It is difficult, though, because we only meet once a week, but I hope somehow we can build up more of a trust."

A student read a powerful piece that sidestepped critical response. No one could translate what they were feeling into workshopese. I asked each student to make a comment and not worry about sounding literary. Still not much, until we got to a student who looked at the author and said, "You're scaring me." The author stood up, walked to the other side of the table, and hugged the "scared" student. Out of bounds? Sure, but it was a remarkable moment that loosened the tension and tightened the class bond.

Workshop Do's and Don'ts

Be there. If you are absent you cannot "make up" the work any more than athletes in team sports can make up games they miss. Even if the teacher allows one or two absences, don't take them as a matter of entitlement; classes should not be cut like excess verbiage. If you are in an academic program, don't tell the instructor that you had to miss class because a history paper was due (unless you would tell your history professor that you missed class because you were writing a poem).

Don't try to establish yourself as the alpha writer. It is not good for you, and it is not good for the workshop. A friend told me that in her first term in a graduate writing program, several students submitted their "greatest hits" for critique, more concerned with establishing themselves as workshop stars than with transforming their writing. They left the workshop with pretty much what they had brought to it. My friend, on the other hand, brought in raw material and left with a chunk of her first novel.

Be on time. Being late for a literature class is disruptive, but Balzac or any Bronte will not suffer. If you are late for a writing workshop, a very alive writer could be hurt if a critique is in progress. Chronic lateness can be infectious, causing critique time to be truncated.

Don't try to establish yourself as the alpha critic. Witty, scathing critiques should be saved for reviews of books by authors making tons of undeserved money. One student was told in class that his writing was "an affront to literature." The workshop is not the guardian of literature; we are door-openers, not gatekeepers.

Be helpful to the teacher in giving everyone an opportunity to speak. In some workshops, a few students tend to dominate the discussions. If you are one of the talkers, you can help by hanging back occasionally.

Don't conflate the I of the piece (or any other character) with the author. Don't think, *What kind of person would write such a thing?* The only transgressions you should hold authors responsible for are their characters' unmotivated words and deeds.

Be a nurturer.
Don't be a coddler.

Be patient and don't make snap judgments about the effectiveness of a teacher or workshop. If you feel frustrated, don't let it hamper your full and open participation; it is hard to learn from inside a shell. The wisdom derived from a class may not take full effect immediately. You may find yourself internalizing a teacher's voice years down the road. This is not to say that the workshop should create a posthypnotic state, where you blindly repeat what you were told, but if you ingest as much as possible during the term, you have a good shot at reaping benefits long after the workshop is over.

Don't be too jealous of any successes by others in the workshop; success can be contagious. You never know where your classmates will wind up, and what they might be able to do for you. This doesn't mean that you won't ever experience an inkling of what Gore Vidal was referring to when he revealed, "Every time a friend succeeds, I die a little." If this schadenfreude-in-reverse ("freudenschade"?) happens, just shrug and think, *Oh, you again*, and offer congratulations.

Be attentive to your classmates' work. Read with care and concern.

Don't belabor a point once it's been made and remade. I was on a jury when an attorney kept hammering home the same nail, until the judge said, "Noted, now move on."

Be communicative with your teacher if you have any significant problems with your writing or with the class.

Don't be intimidated by what your classmates write. There's a chance you may be doing something they can't do. The story goes that a marathon champion met someone at a party who had just run a marathon. The champion asked what the fellow's time was, and the guy sheepishly confessed that he hadn't even broken five hours. The champion replied with admiration, "I can't imagine running for five hours *straight*."

Be generous to your classmates by giving thoughtful comments. A workshop's success is dependent not only on the openness of students to *take* criticism, but also on their willingness to *give* it. Some students are reluctant to say anything they are not absolutely sure of, so they don't say anything. Keep in mind that responses are as much works-in-progress as the pieces under consideration, and our ideas can crystallize through talking. As Gracie Allen said to George Burns, "Do you know that almost everything I know today I learned by listening to myself talk about something I didn't understand."

Don't try to get even. The following note from a student evinced an audible reaction when I read it to the class: "I often feel guarded with my criticism of others' work, for fear that anything too harsh (honest?) might result in a reciprocal attack on my work." Such retaliation is rare, but it can be like a chloroform-dipped rag on the life-breath of the class. Fortunately, the workshop process has a self-regulating feature: other voices are there to dilute the poison. If you do feel attacked, don't react hostilely. Break a pencil point if you want to channel your anger (don't do it with a fountain pen), and try to recast the comment into something useful. If the irritation persists, talk to your classmate or the teacher (but do it outside of class).

Be a good sport. If a classmate gets knocked down with criticism, extend a hand rather than pile on.

Don't keep score. A student came to my office, concerned that I often praised others whose work she considered to be weaker than hers; she feared that it devalued the praise I gave her. I asked her (with a smile) if my being harsher on the work of others would make her feel better. She replied, somewhat embarrassed, that her real concern was whether my praise for her work was sincere. I suggested that if she listened carefully to my comments, she could detect different levels of praise. But, more important, my comments are not only pitched to the general level of the class, but also to the level of each individual, so I might be singing praise in different keys.

Be attentive when your work is being critiqued, and make note of everything said. Follow up on any points that might need clarification or elaboration. The more you sow during the critique, the more you reap when you rewrite.

Don't repeat to outsiders what you hear and read in the workshop; assume that all information is confidential and all pieces are restricted to workshop members unless otherwise stated. This is especially important with material that may refer to the authors' friends and families. (Don't go to Thanksgiving dinner at the home of a classmate and say, "Oh, Aunt Rita, I'm so sorry about the typo on your Elvis tattoo, and does it still hurt to sit down?") I once received a phone call from the father of an upset student. His daughter had never taken a writing class, but her former boyfriend had workshopped a story about their breakup, which was being passed around the dorm.

Be courteous with how you dress your manuscript for school. Unless instructed otherwise: Double-space (except perhaps for poetry); leave wide margins (top, bottom, right, left) for notes; run spell-checker, then proofread the old-fashioned way; place commas and periods inside the closing quotation mark (semicolons and colons, outside); indent new paragraphs (if you do not indent, insert a blank line between paragraphs); number pages (the computer will do this for you, but you must issue the order); don't play with typography—use a basic font (this is a draft, not a brochure); put your name, the title, and the date on the front page, and indicate if the piece is in response to an assignment or is a revision of something previously turned in; fasten with a staple or clip.

Don't let outside relationships enter the workshop. If you know any of your classmates in other contexts, try to neutralize whatever affection or animosity you may have for them.

Be open. Not everything presented by your classmates will be your cup of tea, but your job is to sip from whatever is served. It is often a good thing for a writer to go through a literary-ideological phase, such as eschewing all first-person or present-tense narratives, or declaring "realism rules" or "surrealism is the only response to the wacky world." When the writer's and the respondent's ideologies clash, the critiquer should be receptive. If you do make a comment colored by, say, an aversion to minimalist fiction or anything resembling science fiction, find a way to let the author know that your suggestion is not "This is what I would do if I were you," but rather "This is what you would do if you were me." The workshop puts a solitary act into public scrutiny, turning a solo effort into a group cause. We must not homogenize the individual voices in the room by maneuvering critiques toward a common vision. Rome may have been designed with all roads leading to it, but the workshop is more like an expanded version of Frost's yellow wood, with roads diverging in many directions. Follow your classmates down the roads they choose; you may discover places to return to on your own.

Literary Correctness

The University of Iowa's Norman Foerster said at a conference on creative writing in October 1931: "But we have no right to go on to prescribe the direction to be taken by the writer's energy, the view of life for which he is seeking to find a fit vehicle, the particular *ism* to which he consciously or unconsciously adheres. He must be free to find himself, or to hang himself."

Louis Zukofsky, in *A Test of Poetry* (1948), writes: "Recent critics of literature have expressed the opinion that the beliefs implied or held in a poem influence the reader's appreciation. The opposite opinion would be that a poem is an emotional object defined not by the beliefs it deals with, but by its *technique* and the *poetic conviction or mastery* with which these beliefs are expressed."

Striving for political correctness—usually stemming from a sincere desire to make the world a better place—can be disruptive to the workshop process. How can we try to make and respond to literature if we are squeamish about dealing with race, sex, nationality, and religion?

I admire and value writing that elevates our understanding of contemptible attitudes and actions, such as Eudora Welty's short story "Where is the Voice Coming From?" (written from the point of view of a racist who murders a Civil Rights leader). But if such a piece is not fully realized, it may appear to promote—rather than illuminate—antisocial views. When a writer attempts to expose rather than endorse something despicable, a piece that doesn't quite succeed may offend. Your task in the workshop is the same as with any other piece: help it succeed.

We come to the aid of love poems that don't effectively express love, and death poems that don't truly capture loss. Shouldn't we be as generous with writers who are working with other kinds of volatile material? We wouldn't need the workshop if we could always make successful literary works on our own.

But how do you react to a story that you feel may be purposefully demeaning to any group of people? If a piece has literary intentions and is repellent or offensive to you, it is not out of bounds to let the author know your reaction. (A piece without literary intentions doesn't belong in the workshop.) Even if you feel there is no moral vision or context for the objectionable material, you can choose to work on the piece as a doctor would on a patient he or she dislikes.

This raises a moral dilemma for some: Are you obliged, like the physician, to treat whatever comes before you? Do you want to be responsible for making something "bad" be written well? You can choose not to read Louis-Ferdinand Céline (a brilliant writer with some very unappealing views), but what if a would-be Céline is at the workshop table?

In one instance, a decidedly misogynist story was on the

table. I made eye contact with a student who devoted most of her waking hours to the women's movement. She discreetly shook her head (as if to say, "I'm off duty") and kept quiet during the critique. Another student did address the sexism, and the author responded that he was entitled to his viewpoint. It was tense for a couple of minutes, then I said, "We've established that some people find this piece to be offensive, now let's move on." Most of the class was relieved to have the issue acknowledged and out of the way.

Literature often reflects extremes, and the workshop table may be the best place to encounter them. Whether you choose to respond with silence, brief rebuke, or constructive criticism, you should keep the overall well-being of the class in mind.

A student's choice of persona or setting can also create tension in a workshop. Does a white person have the right to write from a black person's point of view? May a Catholic write about Hebrew school, a wealthy person about homeless people, or a neoclassicist about a deconstructionist?

Consider the case of Danny Santiago, lauded as an up-and-coming Chicano writer with the publication of his 1983 novel *Famous All Over Town*. But *Santiago* turned out to be a pseudonym for Daniel James, a 73-year-old Anglo, who was criticized by those who felt he had no right to appropriate an ethnic identity. Alicia Hernandez had contributed editorial support and encouragement during many years of correspondence with "Danny Santiago." Despite her feelings of betrayal when she learned his true identity, Hernandez concluded, "The work was so authentic that it didn't matter that Danny was indeed White rather than Chicano," and she was told by young Chicano writers that they "credit Danny for being the first to validate the Chicano experience as a source of art."

I think workshops (where writers can't hide their identity)

should let works stand on their own. This doesn't diminish the challenge for the writer. Just because you have the right to take on any persona or subject matter you choose, doesn't mean you won't sound false notes. It is the workshop's job to help get the piece in tune, not challenge your right to play the instrument.

A Fearsome Threesome: Therapy, Sentimentality, and Genre

Writers may fear that a heartfelt autobiographical piece will be dismissed as "therapy." I consider writing to be therapy when it is cathartic for the writer; literary writing occurs when a piece is cathartic for the reader. Can a piece of writing be both? Sure. Can it be therapy without being literary (or vice versa)? Same answer.

What to do in a workshop when a piece does not transcend therapy? Some writers make it easy by declaring, "I don't care if it works for anyone else. It means something to me." My response: "Then you shouldn't bring it to the workshop, where we do care if it works for anyone else."

When a delicate piece appears on the table (by an author open to criticism), we should factor in—a bit more than usual—the author's feelings and the sensitivity of the subject matter. And the author may have to install an extra layer of insulation between the skin and the nerves.

Then we all have to go about our business, which is making the submission as fine a work as it can be.

Sometimes a piece of writing will touch me deeply yet push away another reader, and this is particularly tough when I am the author. (I once received a form rejection slip with a handwritten addendum: "I liked the story, but my Editor would think it too sentimental.") We may have to risk sentimentality to capture true sentiment, but it is worth the risk. Neruda writes, "So much the worse for the poet who does not respond with song to the tender and furious summons of the heart!" Some of my most fulfilling experiences as a writer have occurred answering that summons.

Pianist Keith Jarrett said of his gorgeous CD *The Melody at Night, with You,* "The people who don't get it call it sentimental." A piece of writing might come across the workshop table that crosses the line into sentimentality. Make an attempt to "get it," then try to help get it to the other side of the line.

Kinds of writing (poetry, fiction, nonfiction) are known as *genres,* but references to *genre writing* (mystery, horror, romance) are often unkind. Many genre pieces tend to be superficial and derivative, terrific for diversion and entertainment but with little or no aspiration to literary quality. For a piece to transcend genre, it should have multidimensional characters rather than caricatures who play out preordained roles, and a plot that serves an authentic story rather than a formula.

H.G. Wells and Edgar Allan Poe produced enduring literature before there were such classifications as "science fiction" and "horror." Paul Auster has adapted elements of the mystery genre in his literary fiction; Nicholas Christopher's *Desperate Characters* is a literary *noir* "novella-in-verse"; Kurt Vonnegut transcended science fiction.

As long as the author is striving for literary quality, the workshop should not be hostile to a piece just because it has characteristics of a genre.

Critiquing the Teacher

I approach my classes as I do my own writing: with a mixture of hard work, experience, talent, and trepidation. And, like my writing, what I do is open to collegial criticism. Your teacher may request feedback through in-class comments during the term and/or written evaluations at the end (usually required in academic programs). If your teacher doesn't open the door for suggestions, you may have to knock, gently.

When I solicit feedback—via anonymous notes or open discussion—about what is working and not working in the class, similar comments often wind up on both sides of the ledger. One student lauds the way we deal with each piece on its own terms without judging whether it is "good" or "bad," while another is frustrated because "it is difficult to determine the worth of one's writing outside the womb of the class."

Or:

"Criticism is too harsh." / "It's too nice."

"I like that we read manuscripts in advance." / "I'd rather listen to a story before physically looking at it."

"We spend too much time on any one piece." / "I appreciate the in-depth treatment."

"I want more discussions of craft." / "Craft discussions take away from the workshop's *raison d'être*."

"I want to hear more from my classmates and less from the teacher." / "I'm not paying to hear other students talk so much."

So, if asked, be forthcoming with your suggestions, but appreciate the complex context in which your teacher is working.

Reconcilable Differences

Master violinmakers teach apprentices how to make violins the way they do. This is not usually the case with writers who teach, but it is possible that you will study with someone who is best equipped to teach in his or her own image, which may not be what you want to see when you look in the literary mirror. You and your teacher may have different approaches, such as: You're a magical realist and your teacher thinks that magic should be saved for Vegas lounge acts; or, you love the pronoun *I*, and the teacher would like to gouge your *I*'s out.

These dissonances can be good for you. Listen carefully and apply as much as you can for the length of the workshop term. If only a tad sticks with you, it could give your work a distinctive edge. The singer-songwriter Dion was passing a synagogue and stopped to listen to the cantor; a morsel of what he heard went into one of his early hits, "Donna the Prima Donna."

You can seek out difference by taking a workshop outside of your main genre. Brenda Wineapple points out that Henry James's experience as a playwright (despite his lack of success) had a "salutary" impact on his late novels, as he came to rely less on "explanatory narrative devices" and more on telling his story through dialogue.

Open yourself to influences from other disciplines. John Dos Passos steeped himself in art, music, and cinema.

II

Notes on:
Feedback and Editing

You need a monster editor.

—overheard in a North Beach, San Francisco café,
after the speaker finished reading a lengthy
manuscript by her companion

Prefatory Note: Critique, Not Criticism

A student wrote about being critiqued: "Oh God I'm going to throw up. They hate it, I know they hate it. I should never have raised my hand. Oh God. They like it. I'm going to throw up—what if I write something next week that's terrible? What if I just got lucky? What if they're just being nice? What if they're all secretly laughing at me?"

Which shows that sometimes we can't win for losing, though we *can* lose for winning.

If writers can get thwarted by rebuke, praise, or indifference, what's a workshop to do?

The best we can.

In order to do so, we should distinguish between *critique* and *criticism* (as they apply to the classoom). Criticism is for evaluating and putting into perspective works that have found their place in the world; critiques are for helping pieces get situated. When critique lapses into criticism, the implicit assumption is that what is deficient in the piece will remain deficient. We must see each piece as still growing, and help it grow.

Musicians sometimes introduce a song with, "It goes something like this." Usually this is said by consummate pros playing songs they've performed hundreds of times and, in fact, it goes *exactly* like this. In the workshop, however, the writing has not been refined through years on the road, so it really does "go something like this."

A good critique requires a solid knowledge of language and a sensitivity toward the person writing the language. A well-worded, well-timed comment can send a writer eagerly back to work, while an ill-phrased or ill-placed remark can stop the writer dead in his or her tracks. These stakes are lowered considerably if everyone is aware that all comments have an implied preface of, "You might want to *consider* what I'm about to say." Or, "Here's my comment. It goes something like this."

Bent *Stutzes*, Willie Mays, and Bambi

I was watching a teenage gymnast do miraculous things in the Olympics. Her flexibility and strength were astonishing. Her whole life had led to this moment. The television commentator—a former gymnast—shrieked something like, "Oh no, she bent her knees on the *stutz*! What a tragedy; she was doing so well." I hadn't noticed anything go seriously wrong. Perhaps her knees *had* given a little, but it was amazing that her knees were still attached to her legs.

This brings to mind what Coleridge refers to in *Anima Poetae* as "the head-dimming, heart-damping principle of judging a work by its defects, not its beauties." Yes, we must deal with defects, and it is our obligation to point out our classmates' botched literary *stutzes*, but we must never forget the beauties. And, if you come across that rare and wonderful being, the fully-realized, beauteous piece of writing with nary a bent *stutz*, don't go looking for trouble, fearing that unless you find fault you haven't done your job as a critiquer.

Another way to dim the head and dampen the heart of a classmate is to react with a dismissive *I've seen this kind of thing before* attitude. Something old to you may have just been born in the writer; be gentle with that baby. Even more problematic is *We shouldn't be seeing this kind of thing again.* A poet told me that his first submission to a workshop was greeted with, "I can't believe that anyone still writes poetry that way." *I* can't believe that anyone would say such a thing to a classmate.

When responding to a writer in a "slump," throwing effusive praise on work that the author knows is inferior could do more harm than good. The best way to un-dim the head and un-dampen the spirit is to accept what is before our eyes and encourage the writer to keep swinging. Willie Mays was batting .477 in the minors when he was called up to the Giants in 1951, where he started out 0 for 12. He tearfully told his manager, Leo Durocher, to bench him or send him back to the minors. Durocher replied that Mays wasn't going anywhere: "Just keep swinging, because you're my centerfielder, even if you don't get a hit for the rest of the season." Mays got a lot of hits and was named rookie of the year (he is now in the Hall of Fame). He later recalled, "I think that really, really turned me around."

When my wife was in fourth grade, she came across an oversized, illustrated edition of *Bambi* in the school library. The sprawling pictures of the forest—with their sweeping colors and expressive faces on the animals—enchanted her, and she excitedly cradled the book and went to the desk to check it out. Her teacher stopped her cold with, "Isn't that a little young for you, dear?" She returned the book and didn't tell her parents about it, embarrassed that she had selected a childish book. I can picture her expression as she tried to cover up the rebuke she felt. She got over it, and there were many more books for her, but she never quite trusted that teacher again. We must help one another tap into enchanted places, not plug them up so that nothing more can pour forth.

Classified Comments

I have classified literary feedback as *reactive, descriptive, prescriptive*, and *collaborative*. These categories overlap, and usually a teacher, editor, or classmate will respond with more than one type. If you have respondent's block, you can run through the categories and see if something comes to mind.

Generally speaking, specific comments are best, but at times a general reaction may be called for. In **reactive** feedback, one offers a general, unsubstantiated response: "This paragraph is very moving." "I have some trouble with the dialogue." "The restaurant scene is funny." Rimbaud was known to yell out a reactive *"Merde!"* when a poem of which he disapproved was being read. (He was a poetic genius but we might not want him in our workshop.)

Favorable reactive feedback can encourage a writer to keep going. William Maxwell's novel *The Folded Leaf* started as a short story, which he showed to Louise Bogan, who suggested he expand it into a novel. He sent her chapters as he wrote them, and, he recalled, "from time to time I got a penny postcard from her with 'v. good' or something like that on it."

Reactive comments can be frustrating. One student described a session full of them: "'Well, this was soft,' 'that was phony,' and 'the little thing you did with the doohickey just didn't work.' Thanks a lot. I'll keep that in mind." And Anne Sexton was put off by her husband's response, "I don't think that's too hotsy-totsy."

I believe that the problem with many reactive comments lies not in someone *making* them, but in no one else making anything *out* of them. Comments like "this is terrific" or "this doesn't work" can be starting points for discussing why and how something is terrific or doesn't work. One respondent might not be able to do more than point out a troubled area, but another student (who perhaps didn't originally see the problem) might come up with a solution.

One barometer for the success of a piece can be whether or not respondents are able to articulate what is going on; but much wonderful literature is evocative yet baffling, impossible to explicate while inexplicably packing a wallop. Or, so simple (yet potent) as to not engender copious analysis and debate. Reactive comments may be especially appropriate for writing that eludes critical commentary or wilts when subjected to line-by-line scrutiny.

Descriptive feedback goes a step further and describes what the writer is doing well or not-so-well: "The dialogue reflects the inner lives of the characters" or "I can't figure out when the flashbacks are taking place." It is up to the writer (or a classmate) to figure out what to do about it. One of Louise Bogan's postcards to William Maxwell "objected to a physical description, on the ground that the writing wasn't very fresh, so I sweated over it." Legendary editor Maxwell Perkins, in responding to a draft of Marcia Davenport's novel *East Side, West Side,* wrote to the author: "I do have some fear that the murder runs too far toward melodrama."

Prescriptive feedback offers concrete suggestions for change. The descriptive comment "You have too many characters," might be followed with, "Get rid of the cousin and combine the two brothers." If you feel a passage is overwritten, you might suggest specific words or phrases for the author to consider deleting or tightening.

Prescriptive feedback also includes suggestions for additions. A student wrote in a story "I tried to stop him," and I suggested that the author show *how* the narrator tried to stop him (with gestures, words, violence?). In another story, a character we haven't met conveniently drops by before 8 a.m. and mediates an argument. I suggested that the character be a house guest who has been woken up by the argument.

For *East Side, West Side*, Perkins suggested that Davenport put an orchestra on the Staten Island ferry to play "some old-time song" for Jessie and Mark. In the published novel, an accordion-player performs a "wheezy"-sounding "The Sidewalks of New York." William Maxwell got stuck while writing *The Folded Leaf*, and Louise Bogan sent him a prescription: "Get that boy up off the bed on the sleeping porch."

Prescriptive feedback can be structural. An early draft of Mary Gordon's *Final Payments* was written in third person, and Elizabeth Hardwick suggested that Gordon change it to first person. About the editing of *Presumed Innocent*, Scott Turow told an interviewer: "I had written a single chapter describing Rusty's past relationship with Carolyn, and [Jonathan Galassi] suggested chopping it into three and interspersing it because it was a hard gulp."

For one of my stories, my wife said, "Make them happy longer"; about another story, a friend prescribed "some more oomph." Yes, these prescriptions are vague, but we can't—and shouldn't—always be spoon-fed. Such remarks can give a writer the impetus to return to the private struggle.

Some prescriptive comments border on collaboration. I define **collaborative** feedback as occurring when the respondent supplies an essential idea or contributes significant language to the text (often by inserting or substantially rewriting sentences). A student's story, set in a bar, was told by a nebulous third-person narrator; much of the story was fascinating but incredulous. I suggested that the story be rewritten from the point of view of the bartender, who could be telling the story as a slightly tall tale (as some bartenders are wont to do).

Not every word in a published piece has necessarily been written by the name in the byline. *New Yorker* editor Harold Ross wrote "bucks" for John Cheever during his editing of "The Enormous Radio." In the story, a diamond is found after a party; according to Cheever's recollection of the editing process, a character says, "Sell it, we can use a few dollars." Ross replaced *dollars* with *bucks*, which Cheever found "absolutely perfect. Brilliant." Collaborative feedback, of course, should be on a take-it-or-leave-it basis, and Cheever rejected many of Ross's other suggestions. The last three words of a story of mine published in *The New Yorker* were penciled onto the manuscript by my editor. I accepted them, and they became mine (a non-returnable gift).

Fiction writer Lucia Nevai recalls Eileen Schnurr, an editor at *Mademoiselle*, changing "Clay, he announces" (spoken by an excavator) to "Clay, he pronounces." Given the context, Nevai felt "just that word, with its innuendo of marriage, was a poetic improvement for which I was very grateful."

Ron Padgett provided a similar service while editing an essay of mine. Struggling to express that I didn't feel a conflict between teaching and writing, I wrote: "But the public act of teaching and the private act of writing rarely clash with each other, and mesh often enough to make the slash between writer/teacher a point of coming together rather than a foreboding border." Nice thought, bad execution. Revisions can consist of adding, deleting, or changing words, and Ron did all three in the second half of that sentence: " . . . and mesh often enough to make the slash between writer/teacher a meeting point rather than a barrier."

Barrier was absolutely perfect. Brilliant.

On a more lofty and influential level, Thomas Jefferson wrote, "We hold these truths to be *sacred and undeniable*," which Benjamin Franklin changed to *self-evident.*

The mere proposal of collaborative feedback can propel the author to find his or her own solution. Editor Beena Kamlani said that after she rewrites a problematic passage, "an author might say, 'But that's not the way I want to say it,' and then go ahead and do it exactly the way they want to do it."

One of my students wondered if she could "take credit" for a piece that had been vastly improved as a result of prescriptive and collaborative feedback, and I replied, "Sure you can; it happens all the time. I heard about a writer who erases editorial comments so there will be no trace of another's input." This might not have bothered Maxwell Perkins, who told his wife that he saw his role as "a little dwarf on the shoulder of a great general advising him what to do and what not to do, without anyone's noticing."

The best feedback is often a weave of different types. David Ignatow responded to a story of mine with some reactive words of praise to soften me up, followed by a descriptive comment: "The conception of speeding towards forgiveness and renewed openness is just a bit too simple for what you have brought to the surface." He closed with the prescriptive: "I think the character should stumble here and there in his rush to change."

There's a fifth option: **no feedback**. If we don't connect to a piece, we shouldn't strain for comments because we feel we need to say *something*, the writer might take such responses more seriously than he or she should. An editor once rejected a story of mine without his customary comments, writing: "It's just out of my line of vision." I appreciated that (once I got done *not* appreciating it). Since most workshop comments are self-generated (rather than in response to being called on by the teacher), you can occasionally do the physically but not metaphorically impossible: sit on your hands and hold your tongue. If your teacher does call on you, play it low-key—as new doctors pledge: "First, do no harm." Perhaps use your time to ask questions.

Sometimes a writer merely needs to hear how the work sounds. You can get together with classmates for out-loud sessions, reading new work without critiques. You may not even need your classmates: John Steinbeck tried out material on his dogs. He said Angel sat and listened, but he felt that Charley "was just waiting to get a word in edgewise." (And a "red setter chewed up the manuscript of *Of Mice and Men*.")

A Note on Notes

A student frowned at my editing marks on her manuscript and said, "I'm making too many mistakes." I showed her the edited manuscript of a published story of mine and pointed out all my "mistakes."

When I was in high school, such markings (usually done in blood red, which never bothered me because I like red) were known as *corrections*; in the workshop, I prefer to call them *notes* or *emendations*. Many workshop teachers require students to make notes on one another's manuscripts; if not, you may still choose to exchange written responses.

Word choice is particularly crucial in writing response notes. *Nice* is a useful word that is often considered to be damning-with-faint-praise, but I have tried to rehabilitate *nice*, using it as an adjective followed by an exclamation point, as in: "Nice image!" Another word that can leave a writer cold is *interesting*, but I value any writing that maintains my interest; as with *nice*, I am trying to enable *interesting* to lead a helpful editorial life. I will continue to exile *trite* and *corny*. (When a student was told that her piece was "corny," I tried to salvage the situation by adding, "Yes, in the sense of 'fresh off the cob, hot and sweet.'")

Most writers can best be helped when notes point out flaws within a positive and/or self-deferential context. See how poet Louis Zukofsky phrases his notes on a manuscript by William Carlos Williams: "Here y'are! Don't accept the detailed criticisms in the manuscript unless it verifies your own misgivings, doubts, etc." "I've written on the manuscript lightly so it can be erased & you can still use the copy." "The verse is excellent. But I think it would gain if the ideas it presents were not frequently repetitious." "There is some of your finest writing here embedded in a discursive form which still doesn't form a setting."

When criticizing a problem in a manuscript, if possible point to a place where the author did the same thing well. ("You're vague here, but in the third paragraph on page four you have a wonderful detail.") This will help the author understand the concept and also serve as evidence that he or she is capable of responding to the suggestion.

To make sure my comments are not taken as edicts, I often intersperse them with such "soft" words as *try, perhaps, maybe, see what happens, a bit, a tad*. (As in, "Try to keep the piece chronological and see how it works. Also, perhaps the ending is a tad unclear.") I like using question marks. It is easier to respond to a question than a demand: "Can you combine these two characters?" rather than "Combine these two characters." I might say "Would this character do this?" rather than "The character wouldn't do this," even if I am pretty sure the character wouldn't do this. Sometimes I am truly uncertain: "Is this her idea of what he is thinking, or actually what he is thinking?"

Negative comments can work well in the first person ("I don't grasp this" rather than "This doesn't make sense"), leaving open the real possibility that it is the respondent—rather than the author—who is not grasping it.

It is important not only to suggest changes, but also to recognize what is working. Using reactive phrases (*strong detail, I love this, makes me smile, it's terrific how you used a flashback here*) is the equivalent of responding *I hear you!* when a friend says something important and you want to acknowledge that you get it.

The tone of your comments will depend partly on your relationship with the author. If you have a good rapport, you might be able to employ bluntness. Kurt Vonnegut wrote "reads junky" next to a paragraph in one of my stories, and I was flattered, taking it as a sign of respect. (And the fact that he only wrote it next to *one* paragraph made it an exception that proved the rule of not-junky writing.) The word I typically use in "reads-junky" situations is *recast*, meaning the conception is there but the execution is, as a couple of my English teachers used to write, *awk* (for "awkward"), which I found to be disheartening.

One of the most common forms of written feedback is the bracketing of possible deletions. I tell students that a bracket means *read the passage without these words and consider deleting them*. I'll indicate if I think something needs to replace the bracketed words.

Here is a montage of some of my written notes. (I worked hard on these, but I never thought they would get published.)

Can you slow down the narrative here—same action, more words?

Rather than her "not paying any attention to the black Labrador at her feet" might it be better for her to pay perfunctory attention: a quick pat on the head, a nudge with her foot?

I like the repetition of "new house."

Get here quicker.

If she is going to play a big part in the crime, then we should get to know her a little more.

Can you find another word here? "Heaves" has unintended connotations.

I like the first stanza the best. You could leave it at that or incorporate two or three phrases from the second stanza into it. I've underlined some possibilities.

I love this paragraph but perhaps it could be part of a different piece—maybe a personal essay.

The lengthy conversation they have on the phone before the meeting would be more effective if it took place at the meeting—you'll have more resources, such as body language and background.

The influence of money. Few people know what it's like to have and to spend such great amounts of money. How was it managed, how was it spent? How did you relate to money after growing up without a lot of it? More about his assistants.

I may have suggested too many deletions; play around with tightening this to its optimal size.

Powerfully understated.

You're trying something very difficult and need some tweaking to pull it off.

Go right from "soapsuds" to "sidewalks."

The loaded words like "purity" and "innocence" dilute the best images.

Dosage

Respondents need to consider how large and frequent the dosages of criticism should be. A student asked me to "write all over" her manuscript, and she was able to handle it, but other writers can only absorb so much on any given draft. For them, feedback should be administered like time-release pills; it is more effective to offer fewer notes on more drafts.

George Balanchine, commenting on how he responds to dancers, said, "If it's a young person I let her do it the first time. I don't tell her everything—it's impossible to do that. I'll say, 'If you do a little bit more turnout, then let's see what will happen.' So next time she'll turn out a little more, and I say, 'Now you're looking very good, but that's not everything. Why don't you look straight and go this way instead of that way?' That's what we do."

And that's what *we* do.

Writing Under the Influence

Respondents sometimes compare a submission to another author or work; such allusions may incite pleasure or pique, depending on whether the comparison is invigorating ("resonates with echoes of Marquez"), invidious ("reeks of Lorrie Moore"), or downright accusatory ("you ripped this off from Barthelme"). WUI ("writing under the influence") should not be considered a violation. Even a certain amount of imitation helps a writer grow, and we don't want to stunt that growth.

The line between appreciating and appropriating (emulating and embezzling) is a fine one. Coincidental similarities with work not known to the writer are entirely possible. And, in rare cases, a lifted phrase or concept may be caused by a bout of cryptomnesia (not being conscious of the similarity between something you write and something you once read or heard), a condition that well-read people are particularly susceptible to.

Peer Editing

Editors help writers conceive, shape, and revise their work; editing can begin before a word is written and end with the final set of galleys. Much about the editorial process is similar to what goes on in the workshop, the main distinction being that in editing for publication the piece is of primary concern, while the development of the writer is more important in the workshop. Not every piece brought to class is going to reach its full potential, but the author should grow a little with each submission.

You may want to team up with a fellow student and serve as each other's peer editors, meeting in informal settings on equal footing. (Your teacher might prefer that you do this after a piece has been workshopped, or for a piece that is not coming to the workshop.) You can exchange manuscripts, with cover notes containing questions and concerns; return them with comments and editing suggestions; and follow through with a face-to-face session for amplifications and clarifications. (These sessions tend to go beyond the piece being considered into larger discussions of writing.)

Differing approaches and clashes of opinion can fuel rather than enervate the peer-edit. One student reported that her editor "showed me what kind of forest I'd created while I redrew the veins on the leaves of her trees." Her editing partner said that the suggestions she received "made me a crazy person" but also "made my creative energies rev." (At the end of one session, the editorial relationship morphed into "personal editing" when one of them asked for advice on which belt she should wear on her date that evening.)

If you have the time and inclination, you may wish to replicate the full-scale editing process, which can happen in three phases (similar to the way a piece goes through drafts): substantive editing, line editing, and copyediting. (As with writing, one's approach to editing should be flexible rather than reflexive.) During substantive editing, the piece is looked at as a whole, with suggestions involving such issues as pacing, characterization, general use of language, and scenes to be added, deleted, or substantially modified. After the author has responded to these suggestions, line editing focuses on the manuscript sentence by sentence. In many cases—especially for a shorter work—substantive and line editing are combined. The final step is copyediting, and the peer edit is an ideal setting for this crucial and consuming task.

A good copyeditor paves the way so that the reader will not stumble on misspellings, grammatical errors, clunky syntax, or poorly placed punctuation. William Bridgwater defines copyediting as "basically the mechanical marking of a manuscript so that it is in literal and literary form ready to go to a printer." He cautions: "If the task sounds easy, you do not understand it."

Bridgwater points out that "unusual" employment of punctuation "has a long and honorable tradition. Punctuation is part of the text." This lesson was impressed upon the editors of a literary magazine when they inserted a couple of dozen legal but illegitimate commas into a short story without consulting with the author, who complained that her "peculiar perspective" had been removed and a "plodding comma-ridden personality" grafted onto the story. The editors issued an apology and reprinted the story, sans extraneous commas, in the next issue.

Copyeditors often make suggestions to tighten the language, striving not to compromise voice in the interest of economy. Copyeditors are vigilant about suggesting corrections for grammatical errors and dubious syntax, but they weigh accepted usages against a piece's literary intentions. If something appears wrong, they consider whether the author might have a reason for it.

Copyeditors must know a lot but act as if they have little confidence in what they know: Even a scintilla of doubt should lead to a consultation with a reference book or the author. In a story about a tightrope walker, the author wrote that the wire is "150 feet above the ground" and, a few pages later, the performer "plunges 100 feet." A secure editor might have changed the plunge to "150 feet"; the appropriately insecure editor queried, "Was there a net?"

Copyeditors don't have to be discreet about informing the author about the discrete difference between *discreet* and *discrete*, but shouldn't chastise or condescend. Every error found adds to their job security.

Copyeditors look for factual errors and inconsistencies. Even Jack Kerouac, hardly one who delighted in being edited, appreciated the discovery of "logical errors, such as dates, names of places." Isak Dinesen received such assistance from her stenographer while dictating *The Angelic Avengers*: "I'd start one day by saying, 'Then Mr. So-and-so entered the room,' and the stenographer would cry out, 'Oh dear, but he can't! He died yesterday in chapter seventeen.'"

Being conversant with the language of editing notation is crucial. You need to know that a slash across a capital letter means *change to lower case* not *delete*, or that a series of dots under a crossed-out phrase means *never mind—leave it in*. You can find a guide to proofreading notations in most dictionaries. I have concocted a short version (see Appendix IV).

If a piece is not far enough along for comprehensive editing, you can compress the process into a *shorthand edit*. Overwriting, vagueness, telling-not-showing, etc., can all be appropriate in drafting a piece, so go easy on them.

A compliment can be given quickly with an exclamation mark, and a problematic passage might be indicated with a question mark. Yes, a question mark is about as vague a response as one could give, but it forces the writer to look closely at the text to see what might be amiss. I once encountered a question mark on an edited manuscript, and I reworked the paragraph, glad that I had been encouraged to look at it again. Then, I noticed that the editor's question mark had actually been placed near a question in the text that I had *ended with a period*.

A side note: Some editors and teachers are reluctant to copyedit poetry. I don't buy that. Poems should get the same editorial attention as any other piece, as long as one is sensitive to the linguistic liberties and devices available to poets. A poet told me he owed the success of a poem partly to the copyeditor who added a comma. That copyeditor might have been reluctant to make such a suggestion to Muriel Rukeyser, who would rubber-stamp (in red ink) in the margins of her poems: *Please believe the punctuation.*

III

Notes on:
Being Critiqued

Very very strange it is to have what I wrote analyzed as I had analyzed good authors. To have them holding the paper, lifting the first page around the back of the second page. Also strange to have them holding something very intimate to me. Very nerve-racking, wringing hands under the table, elation at praise.

— workshop student

Prefatory Note: The Frog in the Bottle

Flannery O'Connor told students at Hollins College, "Every time a story of mine appears in a freshman anthology, I have a vision of it, with its little organs laid open, like a frog in a bottle." O'Connor was referring to the tendency of literary criticism to veer more toward dissection than enjoyment, but a former classmate of hers at the Iowa Writers' Workshop, Jean Wylder, was "sure she was remembering those Workshop sessions at Iowa."

No matter how supportive the workshop, there are moments when the discussion might feel like dissection, and, unlike an anthologized author, you are actually in the room while the examination takes place. But: this frog can get better.

The critique is not an autopsy. You should take it in the spirit of "This is how the piece can live," not "This is how it died." Critical comments provide opportunities to get that frog up and hopping.

A student received a bucket full of praise with a few dollops of criticism, yet she was "devastated" by the words of reproach. I told her: "Isn't it nice to know that a piece you think is terrific can actually be *better?* This is why you are here. Would you really want to invest time, money, and soul into a workshop and leave with what you brought in?"

The Optimal Time and Piece

Robert Graves and Alan Hodge wrote a book for writers called *The Reader Over Your Shoulder.* When you write your first draft, keep the reader out of the room. When you've reached a comfort level, you can let the reader in. At the workshop, the reader is not only over your shoulder but may be nipping at your feet, so it is important to choose the right time to bring a piece to the table.

Exposing a draft when it is too hot can leave you burned, while waiting too long might result in the piece becoming frozen and tough to thaw. If you cannot separate yourself somewhat from the material (or pretend to do so) and deal with it at arm's length (though no further), then it might not be ready for public scrutiny.

Waiting a week or so after last touching such a piece may enable you to be more open to suggestions. After an exhausting bout with a story, you may feel that this is the best you can do and become discouraged at even the slightest hint that it's not enough. A student showed a friend a story she'd just put everything into, and felt deflated when her friend responded, "It's great, just needs some tightening." But some writers are better off getting a piece to the workshop sooner rather than later: when they write for themselves, they write for their harshest critic.

Think of it like selecting fruit: submit a piece for critique just before it feels ready to be consumed.

Productive Pain

Being critiqued can be painful. For Ernest Hemingway, it was a pain in a specific place: He gave a draft of *A Farewell to Arms* to F. Scott Fitzgerald, who responded with ten pages of handwritten notes, at the bottom of which Hemingway scrawled his three-word response, "Kiss my ass," signed "EH." According to Dorothy Parker, Robert Benchley was appropriately dismissive (and a bit more civil) when *New Yorker* editor Harold Ross wrote "Who he?" next to a mention of Andromache in Benchley's piece. Benchley wrote back: "You keep out of this."

A better role model for the workshop might be Marcia Davenport's gracious response to Maxwell Perkins: "You make the work almost do itself. I think if I had to struggle alone I would give up."

We have to accept that there will always be injuries caused by critical shrapnel lodging in authors' egos. But when it comes during a workshop it's like hearing bad news from an accountant during tax preparation, as opposed to the worse hurt from an IRS auditor. Either way you pay a price, but the latter comes with penalties. Better to hear it from the workshop, while you can still revise, than to hear it from a critic.

Perhaps writing students should go through a workshop boot camp featuring ego-toughening exercises: Recruits take turns reading a piece out loud, interrupted every couple of lines by a chant of "Needs work! Doesn't work! Needs work! Doesn't work! Needs work!" Then recruits read what they consider to be the best piece they've ever written, and have it be met by silence, paper shuffling, furtive looks at watches, and finally one comment: "It's easy to read. What font is that?"

Or, students could borrow a technique from my childhood dentist. When the drilling got too painful, I'd hold up a finger and he'd ease off a little. When it got unbearable, I'd hold up two fingers and he'd pause so I could regroup.

Since neither of the above is likely to happen, you'll have to grin and bear it, or just bear it. A helpful critique may not be pleasurable, but it doesn't have to be unpleasant. I overheard a student after one of my classes being asked how her workshop went. She replied, "I was kicked around the room." I was about to comfort her when she pumped her fist and added, "It was *great*."

If you can't muster such enthusiasm for being kicked around the room, you might think of it this way: If you are trapped in a well and call for help, you don't want someone to drop down a comfortable chair; you want a rope, even though the climb up won't be fun for either of you.

Get to Know Your Rabbits

The title of Brian De Palma's early movie *Get to Know Your Rabbit* refers to the advice that the teacher of a class for tap-dancing magicians—played by Orson Welles—gives to his students. The rabbits you need to get to know in the workshop include your teacher's and classmates' styles of feedback, and how you tend to react to criticism.

A critiquer's style may be combative and prescriptive or gentle and descriptive, with little variation for specific pieces and authors. If a teacher or classmate typically issues comments wrapped in barbed wire, you shouldn't be cut by them, any more than you should be elated when a respondent with rose-colored glasses tells you how sweet your poem is. Other critiquers employ the approach of the psychotherapist who told me that rather than being a Freudian or a Jungian, he was a *Smithian* when he was treating a patient named Smith and a *Jonesian* with a Jones in the chair.

Monitor your reactions. When I was a workshop student, I found that my initial reaction was to be resistant and petulant; after cooling down, I'd be able to truly consider the suggestions. Even now, as someone critiques a new piece, I may feel myself regressing. If I smile, it might be because part of me is thinking horribly delightful immature responses (such as Thomas Wolfe's first reactions to some of Maxwell Perkins's suggestions: "No, Goddamn it!" and "To hell with it!"). Meanwhile, another part of me is storing the comments for when I grow up once again.

Some writers are resistant to *flattering* comments, simultaneously devaluing their own writing and the respondent's critical acumen: *I'm a bad writer and you're an idiot for thinking otherwise.* Don't discount the notion that there may be something more to what you wrote than meets your own eyes. It's a good time to be wrong.

I knew a psychologist who ran group therapy sessions. Whenever he was asked how it went, he would respond, "It's always good." Perhaps he was overcompensating, but there's a lesson here: For a good student of writing, there is no such thing as a totally bad critique. Though it may not be "always good," you can always get some good from it.

Comment and Effect

Any comment that stops you cold is a bad comment (which doesn't mean it was made by a bad commenter); we can't avoid these remarks, but we can try to file them away. Any comment that keeps you going is a good one (always made by a good commenter). A novelist told me that her outlook changed when a teacher admired the "dark strain" in her work. She had previously been stifled by being told her work was "depressing" or "so sad, are you all right?" A "dark strain" sounded more literary.

The narrator of F. Scott Fitzgerald's autobiographical story "Afternoon of an Author" reveals: "It was like in the beginning fifteen years ago when they said he had 'fatal facility,' and he labored like a slave over every sentence so as not to be like that." I can vividly remember isolated remarks made to me that helped or hindered my growth as a writer; those who made the comments may barely remember *me*, much less what they said. An editor of the college literary magazine doesn't know that when he dismissed my e.e. cummings-influenced poems (sophomoric efforts in my sophomore year) by saying, "I don't like word games," I stopped writing poetry for two years. My fault, for sure, but he hadn't helped.

When I started again, I mustered the courage to show my spare, heartfelt poems (no razzle-dazzle) to David Steinback, a young member of the English department. A dismissal by him might have broken my spirit, but he said some nice things and told me how much he liked the poems. I was halfway out the door when he added, "I don't want you to misunderstand. These poems are not *good*—not by critical standards. But I sense in them that you can be a good poet."

This was the most important combination of comments ever made on my work. With all praise and no qualifiers, I might have continued at the same level, believing I was writing good poetry; or, I might have disregarded his reaction altogether, knowing deep down that success couldn't have come so quickly. Instead, I left feeling slightly discouraged that I hadn't emerged from my shell as a full-blown poet, but excited about what might happen if I kept at it.

I kept at it.

*   *   *

Sometimes we need to make a bold change in our writing. When I was in Michael Goldman's workshop, someone (not in the class) commented that my poems tended to be "too crafty" and that they suffered "from not enough exploration of where they could go from there." I told Michael that I had been *trying* to write very controlled, tight verse, but I was feeling the limitations of the form. My question to Michael was, "Should I just continue to do what I'm doing and naturally expand, or should I make a conscious effort to try new things, through exercises and the like?" Michael responded, "A combination of both," and he added, "The result may only be to bring you back to short poems, but they will gain from it." The bold change didn't come quickly, but I took the crucial first steps with the support of my teacher and classmates.

The Truth Isn't Always the Best Defense

If a writer rejects suggested changes for a story by saying, "But that's the way it really happened," the response could be "Real life isn't always well written" or "But in real life many *other* things happened to motivate this that aren't in this story."

Much of Kim Wozencraft's first novel, *Rush*, was based on her life, which her Columbia classmates didn't know when they were critiquing drafts. She was sometimes challenged about whether a scene was "realistic." Wozencraft took these comments to heart because, as she later said in an interview, "They were looking at the words on the page, and those words didn't convey it in a believable way."

As Nabokov says, "To call a story a true story is an insult to both art and truth."

Not Gospel

Don't take any comments as gospel, nor even be sure that speakers have expressed themselves clearly or have fully formulated their opinions. We talk theoretically; the author decides when to turn theory into practice. This concept makes it easier for authors to absorb comments without being defensive. And—perhaps even more important—it allows respondents to be responsibly bold, knowing they can't actually change anything other than the author's mind.

A workshop is like a jury, in that a single voice can carry much weight; the author chooses which way to tip the scale. One student, happy with a suggestion I'd made, said, "Ten people told me no; you told me yes, so I did it."

A student wrote that his classmates' comments enabled him to "gain the insight to look at a piece of work I was terribly attached to and, like an old tormenting friendship, tell it to get lost, that there's no point to it; and I gained the confidence (or hubris may be more apt) to keep something I had been criticized repeatedly for, not out of stubborn egotism but from a deep seated personal conviction regarding its value."

The above paragraph, for me, comes pretty close to gospel.

Weighing the Responses

Some students tend to rewrite *for* the teacher, aiming to please the authority figure, be it for a grade or approbation. It is only natural that you would place a high value on the teacher's opinions, but you shouldn't accept the instructor's every comment as fiat any more than you should reject, out of hand, classmates' comments because "they're only students." The ultimate arbiters of any piece of writing are readers, and readers often disagree.

The workshop is comprised of careful readers: Pay attention to all and give provenance to none.

Some writers tend to accept criticism uncritically. Someone says, "I wonder about this image," and the student crosses it out without blinking, or someone suggests, "Could this be set in the 1920s?" and the author is on the way to the library. This kind of reaction will only inhibit a free-flowing critique, as it gives unwanted power to the respondents. Then there are the stubborn folks who tend not to do anything suggested by someone else. Try to find the "sweet spot" in between.

Think of it this way: When you entertain guests at a party, you're nice to everyone, you listen, you ask and answer questions, and later you decide whom you might like to have lunch with and whom you might not want in your house again. Similarly, "entertain" *all* suggestions during the critique. Then make your choices.

Even rejected suggestions—if fully considered—can be helpful. One student pointed out that comments she declined to act on "helped me think about what the character is *not* as well as what she is." There are rare cases when no substantial changes result from a critique. In the opening credits to *Happy Days*, Henry Winkler's Fonzie, comb in hand, looks into the mirror then shrugs, choosing not to alter a hair on his head. But he looks.

You can try on changes, and return them if they don't fit. Poet Wendy Salinger received several pages of detailed notes from her editor for her collection *Folly River*. She "accepted all of these & then changed them all back to what I'd originally had because I could never make them sound right in my ear."

You may have a delayed reaction to a suggestion, perhaps when it gets reaffirmed by someone else. Michael Benedikt—then poetry editor of *The Paris Review*—wrote on one of my poems, next to a line about a crazed dog with "an uncocked mouth":

"Alan, this is awfully dangerous, & I'm not sure it's necessary." I rejected his suggestion, and he rejected the poem. Someone else published it, uncocked mouth and all, and I thought I was done with it. Many years later, I included the poem in a new collection. Richard Howard edited the manuscript and he, too, suggested that I remove "uncocked." Now it made total sense for me to do so, and I did.

Sometimes, after a critique and a redraft, a piece still doesn't work. This can be part of the process toward success. The painter Camille Corot wrote in his sketchbook, "One would be wrong to get discouraged after two or three mediocre studies. It is the preparation of the good one that profits, without us noticing so, from this seemingly sterile work." And geochemist David Walker says, "The most important experiments are the ones that go wrong" because there can be much to learn "from understanding why an experiment didn't turn out according to the script."

Or, you may have simply written something unsuccessful and need to move on.

Conference Calls

One-on-one teacher-student conferences are available in many workshops, perhaps through required appointments or drop-in office hours. Conferences provide opportunities to follow up on classroom critiques and discuss your overall progress.

During workshop sessions, teachers must keep all students in mind, but the conference is just for you. You can ask for clarifications or amplifications on any comments you have received, as well as delve into unexplored areas. You can also talk about how you are reacting to the feedback you are getting in the workshop and on the page, so the teacher can best know how to work with you. Conference time is limited, so don't spend it advocating for your work or rehashing what was discussed in class.

The Working Portfolio

Pieces should not be converted to stone—never to be revised—just because the term ends. However, you can take advantage of the impending demarcation line on the calendar to take the work as far as you can.

I suggest that you put together a working portfolio at the end of each workshop, containing your latest revisions as well as drafts, fragments, exercises, and anything in your notebook that might be useful to look at again. The working portfolio reflects the state of your art as the term ends, *and* it serves as a jumping-off point for possible future work.

You can handwrite comments and questions in the margins, or compile them into a cover sheet. It is easier to write such notes if you have an audience: the portfolio can provide the basis for a final conference with your teacher, or you can exchange portfolios with a classmate for an editorial session.

Here is a montage of authorial comments from my undergraduate students' portfolios. Even though the notes are disembodied from the texts, they give a feel for the way the authors were thinking about their work:

> *I added a couple of paragraphs to take some weight off each individual event and give more color to the neighborhood dynamic.*

> *Putting this in present tense made all the difference in showing the experience as new and exciting for the narrator.*

Asterisks: use them or lose them?

It would be helpful to know whether I've made the good choices and have confronted the opportunities. I need to know if the little tensions add up to something, or not enough.

This will be sitting on a distant shelf for a long time while I try to get over the urge to abandon it.

I added one line that I think makes the piece very different in subtle ways.

What about the envelopes? Do they need to open them? Are you distracted by their presence if they remain a mystery?

Narrator—putting him further into the background. No more parentheticals, taming the italics.

No more answering machine messages.

I definitely feel that this piece is still not even close to being finished, but I am content with its progress so far.

I know this is meteorologically necessary, but I think it lessens the impact of the metaphor.

The class found this piece more successful than I had thought it was, which was a pleasant surprise.

Do you think there should be fewer "I miss you's," "I love you's," etc.?

I gave myself a lot of responsibility by making it so wacky, but I never realized that so many ends would have to be tied up to make it feasible.

The entire last scene will probably appear in a different

form, possibly without the involvement of the police, as you suggested.

Another clarity issue I addressed was the setting. By stating she was washing vessels with a hand pump, it physically locates her.

If I am able to discover the word to replace "brooding," then I am sure I will find the title as well.

I changed this to second person narrative—I agree, it works better.

I like that this sentence is long because it "sounds" chaotic like the scene.

Overall I realize this piece is tackling more than I can handle, and I think the focus is lost.

I am struggling with how to manage the off-stage conversation.

I think the "I" needs to enter at that moment.

I want to keep it from becoming one of those "guess who I am or what I am doing" stories.

The Language of Grades

Although many teachers of graduate and noncredit workshops do not issue grades, undergraduate workshop teachers are usually required to do so. It is not fun. I do far more agonizing-per-letter when writing grades than I do for any other work.

Grades comprise a language, and different teachers may speak different languages, with their students speaking yet another. A teacher might define a "*B+*" as *very good*, while a student defines it as *average*. In the teacher's dictionary, "*A*" may mean *excellent, a rare and shining writer*, while a student may put "*A*" in the thesaurus next to *birthright*.

Find out before grades are given what language your teacher speaks. If you are dissatisfied with your grade and want to discuss it with the teacher, the best way is to inquire about the factors that led to the grade, and ask what steps you might take to improve. If you still feel the grade is not appropriate, you can gently offer your opinion, but teachers rarely change grades except for clerical errors.

Six Little Words

It was the end of the last session of my first workshop as a student, with David Ignatow at the 92nd Street Y's Poetry Center in New York. The other students were far more advanced, and I started the workshop slowly. Midway through, I unzipped my lips and began looking forward to the class. By the end, I was downright frightened by the prospect of losing my support team.

Students made their way over to Ignatow to shake his hand and say thanks. I had something else to say, but it wasn't until there were only five of us left that I got out the six little words: "Let's keep meeting on our own." It turned out that the other four were hoping *someone* would say it. So we did.

Six more words: Don't let your workshopmates slip away.

One Word

What do you want to take away from your workshop? I can tell you with one word: *Momentum*.

APPENDICES

I

A Note on:
Being a Writing Teacher

I recall how nervous a student was when she applied to take my workshop, and how she smiled and sighed with relief when I said she could. There was the prospective student who told me, "This is the class I have been looking for my whole life." And the student who showed up at my office on a Friday afternoon (I just happened to be there, perhaps the only Friday that term) to tell me he had made a "bad mistake" in his short story and wanted to correct it. On the last page, he crossed out "faith" and wrote "hope."

Whatever reputation I may have as a teacher is double-edged: some students might perceive wisdom in my pauses, while others might have a "prove-it" attitude. I have been doing this for a long time but I am not sure exactly what it is I do, so I never know if I will be able to do it well on any given day. Mark Twain told a reporter that a bad night on stage shouldn't be blamed on the audience: "It is yourself who is at fault." That's probably not always true, but it can't hurt to act *as if* it is your fault. I try to apply that attitude to my teaching. After a listless session (the worst kind), I will regret that I have to wait another week to make it up to the students.

At some point during the term, the likes of the following may happen: I'll recommend the story *A Country Doctor* but misattribute it to Chekhov (who was, after all, a country doctor) instead of Kafka, and send a correction email in the middle of the night, then worry that I'd said it right in class after all. I'll fret that something I said in jest might have been taken seriously, or that I assumed a student was kidding when she was downright serious. I will cringe remembering a student's name I got wrong. I'll be concerned that the class is too serious, or that I play it too easily for laughs, detracting from the gravitas of the work.

All of that will disappear the next time I walk into the classroom, like turning to a fresh page in a well-worn notebook.

Consider this a public apology to every student to whom I didn't give the needed attention or response. Rest assured it was my failure either to comprehend or communicate. Take Tracy: Hardly a day went by that I didn't see her at school. One afternoon, feeling overwhelmed and under-equipped, I looked up from the jagged strata of papers on my desk and there she was. "I'm sorry, I can't talk to you now," I said. "Come back later." Tracy didn't come back and it wasn't until I was on my way home that I remembered—Tracy had graduated the previous spring.

I will never feel like I have mastered the art of teaching, any more than I will feel like I have mastered the art of writing. In Sherwood Anderson's short story "The Lost Novel," a well-established novelist tells a younger writer, "You almost get at something, sometimes." The two writers agree that no one "ever quite got at—the thing."

I'd be content if my students said, "He almost gets at something, sometimes."

We are sitting around the table, vigorously discussing a short story. The author smiles while his classmates talk about one of his characters as if she were a real person who has just left the room.

I can't help interjecting: "You're all paying to be here and I'm *getting* paid. What a racket!"

II

A Dozen Books

A somewhat arbitrary and by all means incomplete list of some books you might want to have nearby.

1. *The Elements of Style* by Strunk and White and 2. *The Careful Writer; A Modern Guide to English Usage* by Theodore M. Bernstein

The Elements of Style is E.B. White's revised and expanded version of his "English 8" textbook at Cornell (written by his professor, William Strunk, Jr.). The advice is succinct and the examples on target (such as "Halt" and "It was a wonderful show" as examples of, respectively, when to use and not use an exclamation mark). Recently, a Fourth Edition was published with a foreword by E.B. White's stepson, the great *New Yorker* editor and writer Roger Angell, who recalls growing up hearing sounds from White's typewriter come "in hesitant bursts, with long silences in between." The new edition "has been modestly updated, with word processors and air conditioners making their first appearances...and with a light redistribution of genders to permit a feminine pronoun or female farmer to take their places."

Equally grand (and on a grander scale) is *The Careful Writer.* Occasionally, I pick up Bernstein's book to reread his sensible entries on such subjects as *that and which* or *subjunctives* (to name two of the more than 2,000 topics). Bernstein recognizes "the desirability of change" and is flexible in his approach to usage, unlike his fictive foil "Miss Thistlebottom," for whom "it is simpler to lay down a rule than to try to stimulate discriminating thinking." Bernstein insists that we write carefully and correctly "not to satisfy 'rules' or to gratify the whims of a pedagogue, but rather to express ourselves clearly, precisely, logically, and directly," which Bernstein does throughout this wonderful book.

3. *The Oxford English Dictionary (OED)*

Until recently, the *OED* was only available in a room-filling twelve-volume edition or in two mammoth tiny-type volumes that could only be read with the supplied magnifying glass. Now, for those who have access to a subscribing library or can afford the individual subscription fee, it is also online (oed.com), searchable and navigable, and one doesn't have to wait years for a supplement to appear with new words and usages. Beyond the definitive definitions and derivations, the *OED* has 2.5 million quotations illustrating how words have been used. I particularly enjoy coming across obsolete definitions of words—it's like meeting someone's ancestors.

4. *The Deluxe Transitive Vampire: A Handbook of Grammar for the Innocent, the Eager, and the Doomed* and **5.** *The New Well-Tempered Sentence: A Punctuation Handbook for the Innocent, the Eager, and the Doomed*, both by Karen Elizabeth Gordon

Gordon's brief exegeses and quirky samples will refresh what you already know about grammar and punctuation while likely teaching you a thing or two. In *Vampire*, Gordon writes, "The passive voice is appropriate when the action rather than the actor is to be emphasized"; one of her examples is: "The bat suspended from Loona's hair *was repulsed* by her Nuit Blanche perfume." In *Well-Tempered Sentence*, she notes, "Sometimes for easier reading two identical words or words close in sound or appearance should be separated by a comma," which she demonstrates with: "They came in, in striped pants and spats." I also like that Gordon is—as am I—a passionate advocate of using the serial (a.k.a. Oxford) comma.

6. *A Storyteller's Story* by Sherwood Anderson and **7.** *A Moveable Feast* by Ernest Hemingway

Though not reliable as autobiography, these books exude writerly sensibility and mindset. You may not want to write (or live) like Hemingway or Anderson, but these books can make you want to be *writers* like them.

A Storyteller's Story ranges far and wide, with memories (real and imagined) and reflections on writing, told as "Notes" (now, where did he get *that* idea?). In one of my favorites, Anderson writes about finding "sentences and paragraphs that stir deeply," using as an example the story of the Norsewoman Fredis who instigated a mass-killing in Vinland. Anderson imagines the "scribbler"—who risked his life by writing about the murder—being proud of inventing the detail of Fredis waking her husband with her cold feet: "I did rather put a spike into my scene. I nailed it down, now didn't I, Leify old chap."

A Moveable Feast is a memoir of Paris in the 1920s. In the preface, Hemingway writes, "If the reader prefers, this book may be regarded as fiction. But there is always the chance that such a book of fiction may throw some light on what has been written as fact." We will never know what really happened among Hemingway, Fitzgerald, Pound, Stein, and the others, but we know that they were on to something. "After writing a story," Hemingway recalls, "I was always empty and both sad and happy, as though I had made love, and I was sure this was a very good story although I would not know truly how good until I read it over the next day."

8. Aristotle's *Poetics*

Lo these many years (two millennia, three centuries, and ten lustrums) later, these lecture notes show up in the indices of books about literary theory, writing, theater, and film (including a book called *Aristotle's Poetics for Screenwriters*). Even Sam Seaborn on *The West Wing* references Aristotle ("What did he mean? He meant that it's okay to have a broomstick sing and dance but you shouldn't turn on the radio and hear the news report you need to hear"). A few snippets: "The most beautiful colors, laid on confusedly, will not give as much pleasure as the chalk outline of a portrait." Tragedy is stronger when it "is between persons who are near or dear to one another, rather than enemies or indifferent." "The element of the irrational, and, similarly, depravity of character, are justly censured when there is no inner necessity for introducing them."

9. *Editor to Author: The Letters of Maxwell E. Perkins*; John Hall Wheelock, editor

The great editor's letters are models of a knowing mind at work, and are full of grace and wisdom. His letter to Marcia Davenport about her novel *East Side, West Side* is worth the price of admission, a mini textbook on the craft of writing and responding to writing. Other recipients include Thomas Wolfe, Ernest Hemingway, F. Scott Fitzgerald, and Marjorie Kinnan Rawlings.

10. *The Pillow Book* of Sei Shonagon

Not a book on writing, but this millennium-old journal is all about writing. Sei Shonagon, a court lady, was a contemporary of Lady Murasaki (*The Tale of Genji*), who disapproved of Shonagon's aleatoric approach to subject matter: "If one has to sample each interesting thing that comes along, people are bound to regard one as frivolous." But I regard Shonagon as a writer who could convey atmosphere, emotion, and psychology with brevity, humor, and poignancy. Turn to almost any page and you will find something that resonates today and may have you reaching for your own notebook. The highlights of the book are her annotated lists, which include: "Things That Have Lost Their Power," "Things That Gain by Being Painted," "People Who Look Pleased with Themselves," "Things That Make One's Heart Beat Faster," and "Times When One Should Be on One's Guard."

11., 12. *The Paris Review Interviews,* Volumes I and II

The gold standard for literary interviews. Most of the *Paris Review* interviews are available online (parisreview.org), where they are appropriately billed as "the DNA of literature." They have also been collected in several book incarnations; currently, two volumes are available of a projected four-volume "best of" set edited by Philip Gourevitch, who comments in his introduction to the first volume that "for half a century now one of the ways writers learned how to do it, felt less alone doing it, or found affirmation in their solitude while doing it is by observing their fellow writers as they describe themselves at work in the *Paris Review* interviews." We will never have the opportunity to ply the likes of Jorge Luis Borges, Dorothy Parker, or T.S. Eliot with questions, but *The Paris Review* did, and we can revel in the answers.

A side note: If I were asked, "Which three books would you bring to a desert island?" I would go for the *OED*, any collection of *The Paris Review* interviews, and a big, blank, lined notebook.

III

Notes on:
My Writing Teachers

David Ignatow

On February 15, 1971, I received a telegram—a real telegram with the text pasted onto the distinctive yellow Western Union paper—signifying my acceptance into David Ignatow's Craft of Poetry workshop at the 92nd Street Y in New York. I didn't know anything about Ignatow's work, other than that a friend had spoken his name with awe.

That night, I stopped at a bookstore in Penn Station and picked up two of Ignatow's books. As I read his poems about bagels and bums, apples and America, his laments of love and life, I felt like I might have found my teacher.

I wrote a poem about a character named Harvey, and after I read it in the workshop, David said, "You know what William Carlos Williams would have said about that poem: 'So you *know* Harvey, well then *tell* me about him.'" Not only did I have a mentor in David, but now I had William Carlos Williams as a *grandmentor.*

David and I kept in touch, but we had a squabble when I was on the runway of my career, not knowing if I would take flight. On the Richter scale of literary feuds it wouldn't have made a blip, but it was my first one, and David was my main connection with the poetry world. David and I patched things up in the mail, but I was concerned about whether I would ever again be embraced by him. We met by chance at an event. David put his arm around me and said to the others in our circle: "Alan and I have been through some things." David and I would be all right. And, though I may have imagined it, I sensed that the others standing there looked at me as someone on the map.

I was considering graduate school, and I asked David if I could audit his MFA workshop at Columbia. Many years later I would be in the position of turning down such requests out of hand, but David agreed on the condition that I wouldn't submit poems, speak during class, or see him during office hours. I contentedly sat slightly away from the table, soaking up everything without concern at being judged. Not sure if David had officially received permission, I never told anyone I was auditing. A few weeks into the term, David pointed to me and said, "He's the editor of a very important new magazine"; perhaps he had noticed that the other students would go off to bars and cafés without inviting me. After class, I was asked along to the West End.

Good teaching means knowing what to say, when to say it, and how to say it. Here's an example of good teaching. David solicited some of my poems for a section he was editing for *The American Poetry Review*. He sent my stuff back because "you're moving very fast and I want to catch you at your best," asking me to submit new material just at the deadline. How clever: I didn't feel rejected, and I started to write like a maniac. I didn't know how long I might be "moving very fast," and I didn't want to miss a minute of it. (I submitted and he accepted.)

I relied on David's opinions of my work, so it was distressing when I sent him a batch of pieces and he wrote back: "With the exception of two poems, none of these strike me as very good." A few days letter I received an addendum: "I'm sorry to have written you in haste. I was tired that day and low about most things but this morning the poems struck me much more intensely."

A couple of years later, I sent David the proposed manuscript for my first full-length collection, and he replied, "I don't think you have a complete book in this ms." He named 21 poems that "could form the beginning of an excellent book, if you can be patient and continue to write to match these." (I waited, and the book was better.)

I got a note from David when he was working on a new book. "So you'll find my head buried in the typewriter next time we meet. It'll be like I'm wearing a typewriter for a hat." I pictured David writing the first sentence and grinning as the hat image came to him, then continuing to type with utter pleasure.

David gave a reading to a packed auditorium at the Guggenheim Museum. At the reception, I was too shy to wedge my way close to him. One by one, the crowd dispersed, until it was just the two of us. I walked with David out into the frigid, sleeting February night and accompanied him down Fifth Avenue, looking for the bus stop.

I said, "It's quite a compliment that so many people came out to see you in this miserable weather."

"Yes, I'll have to remember that in my will."

We crossed slushy Fifth Avenue. David let a bus go by as we talked. "There are a lot of people who care about your work, and you," I said, my way of telling David that *I* cared about his work, and him.

"Sometimes I forget that."

While David was living in Jamaica, Queens, I had dinner with him in a Chinese restaurant. After dinner, David stopped at a grocery store and paid with a twenty-dollar bill. The clerk examined the bill closely, back and forth, and after it passed inspection he apologized. "That's all right," David said. "It's not *my* money, I just pass it along."

Eventually, I became director of the undergraduate program at Columbia, where David then taught. How awkward this would be for both of us, I thought. David called to ask if he could reschedule a class, several weeks in advance. "Of course. You didn't have to ask," I said, to which David replied, "I always check with the boss."

One August, David—now in his late 70's—called to tell me he had Parkinson's and would not be able to teach anymore because of the strain of the commute from East Hampton. The more awkward my words were, the more comfortingly clever were David's replies.

"I'm sorry this happened," I said.

"*Something* had to happen."

"Well, how do you *feel?*"

"I imagine the way Mr. Parkinson did."

The last time I saw David, he was in the hospital and he was dying. He asked if he could teach the next semester, and I thought for a second that he was delusional, but then he grinned. He had written so many poems about death, I should not have been surprised that he would have some lines prepared. David fell asleep, and I took out one of his books from my bag to show his nurse, to make sure she knew whom she was caring for. David woke up and said to her, "That's my latest book."

When I got the news that David had died, I remembered when he recited one of his poems in our workshop at the Y: "Ignatow is dying / and so is the sun." We stared at him, waiting for the rest of the poem. That was it. David shrugged and said, "Hey, I got it published."

Since David's death, I have kept a wary eye on the sun.

Robert Phelps

For Robert Phelps's course in personal journalism at the New School in 1971, I was writing a series of pieces based on my experiences in the anti-war movement. Once, after class, Robert and I were having coffee in the school cafeteria when we were joined by Marguerite Young (author of *Miss MacIntosh, My Darling*). Robert introduced me and said, "He's writing a book: *Ziegler's War*." That was the first I'd heard of the title, not to mention the book. I wasn't ready to write that book, but I kept in mind that Robert Phelps thought I had a book in me. (I'm still trying to write that book.)

I recall two times when Robert went on tangents during class. Once, he told us with wonder about crossing Broadway near the Columbia campus late at night, how he'd faced north, picturing the land before it was covered with asphalt and concrete, seeing it for the first time as a hill. Another time, he shared with us his dilemma reviewing *The Other*, the first novel by movie star Thomas Tryon. Robert liked the author personally and admired his achievement, but he didn't think the book was totally successful. How could he encourage the author while remaining true to his job as reviewer?

Shortly after the term ended, Robert's review appeared in *Life*, calling Tryon a "first novelist of uncommon finesse, who can prune as shapely a sentence as anyone in the tale-telling business this year." Tryon went on to publish nine more books. He did not appear in another movie.

Joel Oppenheimer

Joel Oppenheimer's private workshop, in 1972, met on the lower floor of his duplex in Westbeth, the former phone company building converted to artists' housing. At the first session, Joel responded to my poem about domestic relationships with, "That's where I live." At a later class, all I had with me was a 21-word poem. Hoping there wouldn't be time for me, I filibustered to keep the discussions going as long as I could. But Joel called on me. I was always amazed at how Joel could come up with ways to discuss a poem—questions to ask, comments to make—but what could even *he* possibly say about this one? I read the poem and cringed.

"Alan," he said, then repeated, "Alan." He shook his head and said, "Helen's got to hear this poem." He called up the stairs to his wife: "Helen, you've got to hear this!" She wasn't there. Joel said he had no suggestions, the poem was perfect as it was. "Leave me a copy to show Helen." What wonderful feedback, to want to share my writing with his wife. After class, as I put on my jacket, Joel put his arm on my shoulder and said, "Alan . . . that *poem*."

Could there possibly be a less erudite, more nonspecific response to a piece of writing? Could a writer dream of a better critique?

A year later, we met up again at the City College graduate writing program. Joel said his goal was to separate the *tummler* (a Yiddish word for an entertainer who "makes a racket") from the *poet* in me. On one of my breakthrough poems he suggested only that I add a "you" (I did) and delete a "so" (I didn't), but his comment on the bottom of the page was crucial: "Good—it works—the old problem we talked about, i think you're getting to it more & more." On another poem he wrote: "Will this ever get written properly? i mean, it's okay now, but you know it ain't down yet. Have you tried this as a story?" Such comments were part of an ongoing dialogue between teacher and student, tailored to *me* first and to the poems second.

Kurt Vonnegut

I had been admitted to the City College program as a poet, but I convinced the director to let me take Kurt Vonnegut's fiction workshop; I wasn't going to be that close to one of my heroes without studying with him.

The workshop met in Kurt's midtown Manhattan townhouse. A few sessions into the term, Vonnegut told us that his writing wasn't going well and he needed to take a week off. He looked pale and dispirited as he explained that he was trying to write about heaven and couldn't figure out how to do it. Two weeks later, when I asked how the writing was going, he smiled, put a thumb up, and said, "A-number one." He looked terrific.

I wrote a short story about rock musicians. Kurt thought it should be a novel. "Are you going to settle for easy victories, be happy with an 'A' in Creative Writing?" he asked me. I would be thrilled with an "A" in Creative Writing from Kurt Vonnegut, but I said I'd give it a go. Kurt added, "Telling you to write a novel is like telling you to get married."

Every couple of weeks we had a one-on-one meeting. Kurt would usually say something before we even sat down. Once, it was "You're on to something," and, later in the term, "You're racking right along. It looks like a book."

After reading a new chapter, Kurt said, "These guys are trouble, get rid of them," about two of the protagonist's band members. I thought he was speaking to me as the author, and I was ready to expunge the characters, but he clarified that he was talking *through* me to the protagonist, who should fire them *in the story.* I felt good; I was creating characters.

My momentum was strong, and Kurt invited me to meet with him after the term ended. A couple of weeks went by, and I mustered the courage to call for an appointment. His wife answered and told me, "The term is over, he's not seeing any students."

Before I could plead my case, Kurt came on an extension and said, "It's all right."

At our meeting, Kurt asked, "Do you know famous rock musicians?"

I told him I'd made it all up.

"Well, this is the way rock musicians will be in a few years."

"Huh?"

Kurt explained that some kid in the Midwest would read my book and become a famous rock musician, emulating my characters because that's all he would know about how a rock musician acts. Then kids would emulate *him.*

Once again, Kurt had made me feel like a real writer.

I asked how his book was going, and he replied, "It doesn't much matter. It's not going very well." I could take that comment two ways: 1) If Kurt Vonnegut has such doubts, who am I to even try to get into the game? Or 2) The fact that I, too, have such doubts doesn't mean I am not worthy of being in the game. (I opted for the latter, which I highly recommend.)

At the end of the session, Kurt inscribed my copy of *Breakfast of Champions*: "For Alan Ziegler, who has begun a book of his own."

Fifteen years later, I sent Kurt the manuscript for a collection of my short stories. I had never finished that novel, but I was happy with my book of "small victories." I asked Kurt for a blurb, figuring I was probably the tenth writer that week to ask him for one—all with connections less tenuous than mine—and that he'd probably long ago forgotten me. I included a return postcard, asking him to check one of five boxes: "I will try to take a look at the manuscript and *maybe* write a blurb." "No, but try again with the galleys." "No." "Yes, but be patient." "It's done. Here's the blurb."

After a week or two, I received the postcard; Kurt had checked the "be patient" box and added, "Just got back from England, so have to catch up on a lot of stuff." In the same batch of mail was an envelope with his blurb, which started out: "I'm honored to know you." I consider those words to be the epitome of kindness.

William Burroughs

William Burroughs had just moved back to New York from London, and it was amazing to see an icon in the flesh, much less have him as a teacher at City College in the Spring of 1974. He agreed to do an independent study with me on my writing, and he gave me permission to tape his undergraduate lectures (which he delivered from typed pages). The first time I put my tape recorder in front of him, I asked if he would release the pause button when he started talking so I wouldn't disturb him. Bill said he preferred me to do it, explaining, "I don't like to fool with other people's machines."

I went a few times to Bill's sparsely furnished downtown loft, which he had just moved into. Usually, he wore a tie. Once, when I arrived he was sitting at a big table typing on an old Underwood; later, he had a new IBM electric. He would serve me coffee and our conversations would be more silence than talk, our cups going up and down.

At one visit, I showed him part of the novel-in-progress that I had worked on with Kurt Vonnegut. He quietly read the piece while I talked with his friend and assistant, James Grauerholz, about small presses. Bill patted his front shirt pocket, making contact with a pack of cigarettes, but he didn't take one.

Bill looked up and asked me the same question Kurt had: "So, you know these rock musicians?"

"No. I made it all up."

Bill said, "It's very, very good. Polished." He paused, and I waited for the *but.* Instead, he asked, "Do you have an agent?"

"No," I replied, my heart beginning to race toward the finish line of a novel with blurbs by Vonnegut and Burroughs.

Bill started coughing and said, "You really need codeine for a cough, but you need a prescription." (The journalist in me recognized the lead: *William Burroughs can't get codeine without a prescription.*) "I know some rock musicians. David Bowie."

"What do you think of him?" I asked, realizing that the lesson was over and he wasn't going to give me the name of an agent.

"Cold and purposeful," Burroughs replied. "Jagger. He's a nice guy and a smart businessman."

We talked about Kerouac and Neal Cassidy. Bill told me that *Naked Lunch* had originated as a series of letters.

As I was leaving, Bill said I should feel free to return. "I'm here in the afternoon."

IV

A Simple Copyediting Guide

All insertions on carets *sit*
Some words must be ~~erased~~/deleted. The delete sign (/) is optional when crossing out.

Large chunks can be circled with the delete sign attached.

Like orthodontists, copy editors close up spaces.
Sometimes just a single letter needs to go, or be replaced.

Sometimes you cast a word aside and want it ~~back~~ *stet*, and, ~~unlike life~~, there are two easy ways to get something back.

Words sometimes need to be separated.
Words sometimes transposed get, as do letters.
a lower case letter can be promoted to a capital.
A Capital letter can be demoted.
Underline three times and all that dwells above will be caps.

Sometimes you want to change your paragraphing.
Sentences in different paragraphs can be joined together. Other times you want to start a new paragraph, perhaps because there's a change in subject matter. Call me Ishmael.

add a comma: ⋀
add a period: ⊙
add a quotation mark: ⱽⱽ
add an apostrophe: ⱽ
change a comma to a period: ⊘
change a period to a comma: ⸲

V

A Visit to The Writers' Chapel

The writers start filing into the chapel, located in a dark café. On the wall are the workshop commandments:

DO NOT TAKE THY WRITING IN VAIN.

REMEMBER THE WORKSHOP DAY
AND DO NOT BE TARDY OR ABSENT.

HONOR THY INFLUENCES.

THOU SHALT NOT MAKE CHARACTERS KILL
OR COMMIT ADULTERY WITHOUT MOTIVATION
OR CONSEQUENCE.

THOU SHALT NOT PLAGIARIZE.

THOU SHALT NOT BEAR FALSE CRITICISM
AGAINST THY WORKSHOP NEIGHBOR.

THOU SHALT NOT COVET THY WORKSHOP
NEIGHBOR'S OEUVRE, ALTHOUGH GUSHY
APPRECIATION IS FINE.

When the room is full, they sit down at Paris café tables, open their manuscript books, and simultaneously bellow an excerpt from a work-in-progress; a joyful noise fills the room.

They turn to the *Book of Common Prose* and read:

> *Oh muses forgive us for we know not what we write. We have only working drafts to show for our trials. We have sinned in our procrastination, laziness, imprecision of language, failure of courage and imagination, and overall lack of will. Please grant us the language to make bad experiences into good stories. Bless us with images, the stubbornness to carry on, the fortitude to forego unjust criticism, and the generosity of spirit to praise the work of others.*

They take communion of a sip of espresso and a symbolic drag on an unlit cigarette. On their way out, some stop by the Confessional Poem booth, where they recite a self-indulgent, autobiographical screed without fear of derision.

VI

A Note on:
The Writing of This Book

I would take it as a compliment if you had the impression that I wrote this book in a few weeks during a break from my "real" writing. But it's not true. This book is as real for me as it gets, and it took years. The manuscript was assembled and disassembled many times; without a deadline, it might have come apart once again.

I had every doubt in the book (including this book). Many times I got stuck on a passage and walked away, ignoring my advice to "finish the line." Sometimes—and I don't quite understand this—I nailed a sentence and walked away. Often, I worked on the book when I was supposed to be doing something else. And there were times when I blocked out time for the book but nothing happened.

I kept revising, expanding, cutting. I maintained a file called *Look*, containing passages I thought might make it into the manuscript (some did, many didn't) and parts I deleted but wanted to reconsider (some got back in, most didn't). The file got so unwieldy that I divided it into *Look*, *Really Look*, and *Really Really Look*. I got feedback; some of the comments made me cranky—these were usually the most useful.

Finally, I reached the point where I felt in danger of revising the manuscript to death by a thousand cuts-and-pastes. I had to let go, knowing that I would be destined to think, many times: *Oh, that should have gone into the book.*

In other words, writing this book was business as usual.

VII

Selected Sources

Anderson, Sherwood. *A Story Teller's Story: Memoirs of Youth and Middle Age.* New York: Viking, 1969.

Ashbury, John. Interview. With Mark Hillringhouse. *NY Arts Journal* Fall 1981: 3–7.

Balanchine, George. Interview. *The New Yorker.* With W. McNeil Lowry. 12 Sept. 1983: 52–88.

Baldwin, Neil. "Zukofsky, Williams, and *The Wedge:* Toward a Dynamic Convergence." *Louis Zukofsky: Man and Poet.* Ed. Carroll F. Terrell. Orono: International Poetry Foundation, 1979.

Baldwin, Neil. *To All Gentleness: William Carlos Williams, the Doctor-Poet.* New York: Atheneum, 1984.

Berg, A. Scott. *Max Perkins: Editor of Genius.* New York: Pocket, 1979.

Brinkley, Douglas. "In the Kerouac Archive." *The Atlantic Monthly.* Nov. 1998: 49–76.

Bruccoli, Matthew J. *Scott and Ernest.* Carbondale: Southern Illinois University Press, 1978.

Carter, William C. *Marcel Proust: A Life.* New Haven: Yale University Press, 2000.

Cheney, Roberta Carkeek. *Sioux Winter Count: A 131-Year Calendar of Events (Traditional Interpretation by Kills Two).* Happy Camp: Naturegraph, 1998.

Cowley, Malcolm. *A Second Flowering: Works and Days of the Lost Generation.* New York: Penguin, 1980.

Darwin, Charles, *The Autobiography of Charles Darwin.* Ed. Nora Barlow. New York: Norton, 1969.

Detro, Gene. *Patchen: The Last Interview.* Santa Barbara: Capra, 1976.

Dillard, Annie. "To Fashion a Text." *Inventing the Truth: The Art and Craft of Memoir.* Ed. William Zinsser. Boston: Houghton Mifflin, 1987.

Doreski, William. "'One Gallant Rush': The Writing of Robert Lowell's 'For the Union Dead.'" *The New England Quarterly* 67.1 (1994): 30–45.

Dylan, Bob. *Chronicles: Volume One.* New York: Simon & Schuster, 2004.

The Epic That Never Was (Disc 5 of *I, Claudius*). Perf. Charles Laughton, Merle Oberon, and Emlyn Williams. BBC, 1976.

Forché, Carolyn. Interview. *The Language of Life: A Festival of Poets.* With Bill Moyers. Ed. James Haba. New York: Doubleday, 1995.

Forché, Carolyn. "El Salvador: An Aide Mémoire." *The American Poetry Review* July/Aug. 1981: 3–7.

Foster, John. *The Life of Charles Dickens.* New York: Dutton, 1927.

Ginsberg, Allen. *Spontaneous Mind: Selected Interviews, 1958–1996.* Ed. David Carter. New York: HarperCollins, 2001.

Goldin, Frederick. *Lyrics of the Troubadours and Trouveres: An Anthology and a History.* Gloucester: Peter Smith, 1983.

Gross, Gerald, ed. *Editors on Editing* Revised Edition. New York: Harper & Row, 1985. [notably, William Bridgwater on "Copyediting"]

Hale, Nancy. *The Realities of Fiction.* Boston: Little, Brown, 1961.

Hayes, Dennis E. "Ships & Such." *Lamont-Doherty Earth Observatory of Columbia University: Twelve Perspectives on the First Fifty Years, 1949-1999.* Ed. Laurence Lippsett. Palisades: Office of Communications and External Relations, 1999.

Hemingway, Ernest. *A Moveable Feast.* New York: Scribners, 1964.

Hernández, Alicia. "Letters and Retrieving the Past: My Involvement with 'Danny Santiago.'" *Life Writing/Writing Lives.* Ed. Bette H. Kirschstein. Malabar: Krieger, 2001.

Howard, Michael S. *Jonathan Cape, Publisher.* London: Jonathan Cape, 1971.

Huidobro, Vicente. *Manifestos Manifest.* Trans. Gilbert Alter-Gilbert. Los Angeles: Green Integer, 1999.

Ignatow, David. "A Poet's Notebook." *The New York Quarterly* 5 (1971): 79–94.

Jacob, Max. *Advice to a Young Poet.* Trans. John Adlard. London: Menard, 1976.

Kafka, Franz. *The Basic Kafka.* Ed. Erich Heller. New York: Pocket Books, 1979.

Kamlani, Beena. Interview. With Jerry Gross. *Fiction Writer* July 1999: 62–66.

MacDonald, Hugh, ed. *Portraits in Prose: A Collection of Characters.* New Haven: Yale University Press, 1947. [John Phillips on John Milton, Lady Blessington on Lord Byron, Sir Francis Darwin on Charles Darwin, C. Venables on William Wordsworth]

Mayakovsky, Vladimir. *How are Verses Made?* Trans. G.M. Hyde. London: Jonathan Cape, 1970.

Moxley, Joseph M., ed. *Creative Writing in America.* Urbana: NCTE, 1989.

Nabokov, Vladimir. *Lectures on Literature.* New York: Harcourt, 1980.

Neruda, Pablo. *Memoirs.* Trans. Hardie St. Martin. New York: Penguin, 1978.

The Paris Review. Interviews with John Berryman, John Cheever, Isak Dinesen, Jack Kerouac, William Maxwell, Vladamir Nabokov, Dorothy Parker, Anne Sexton, and John Steinbeck (located in various editions and online, www.parisreview.org).

Pasternak, Boris. *I Remember: Sketch for an Autobiography.* Trans. David Magarshack. New York: Pantheon, 1959.

Perkins, Maxwell E. *Editor to Author: The Letters of Maxwell E. Perkins.* Ed. John Hall Wheelock. New York: Scribners, 1987.

Plumb, Cheryl. "Revising *Nightwood.*" *Review of Contemporary Fiction* 13.3 (1993): 149–159.

Polya, George. *How to Solve it: A New Aspect of Mathematical Method.* Princeton: Princeton University Press, 2004.

Rees, Ronald. "Constable, Turner, and Views of Nature in the Nineteenth Century." *The Geographical Review* 72.3 (1982): 253–269.

Reid, Alastair. "Neruda and Borges." *The New Yorker* 24 June 1996: 56–72.

Steinbeck, John. *Journal of a Novel: The East of Eden Letters.* New York: Penguin, 1990.

Sternburg, Janet and Alan Ziegler. "A Conversation with Charles Reznikoff." *Montemora* 2 (1976): 113–121.

Stoney, Barbara. *Enid Blyton: The Biography.* Gloucestershire: Tempus, 2006.

Thiele, Leslie Paul. "Heidegger on Freedom: Political not Metaphysical." *American Political Science Review* 88.2 (1994): 278–291.

Tolson, Jay, ed. *The Correspondence of Shelby Foote & Walker Percy.* New York: Norton, 1997.

Tolstoy, Ilya. *Reminiscences Of Tolstoy.* Trans. George Calderon. Whitefish: Kessinger, 2004.

Turow, Scott. Interview. *Conversations with American Novelists.* Ed. Kay Bonetti, Greg Michalson, Speer Morgan, Jo Sapp, and Sam Stowers. Columbia: University of Missouri Press, 1997.

Wilbers, Stephen. *The Iowa Writers' Workshop.* Iowa City: University of Iowa, 1980.

Wozencraft, Kim. Interview. With Jill Eisenstadt. *Bomb* Spring 1992: 30–34.

Wylder, Jean. "Flannery O'Connor: A Reminiscence and Some Letters." *North American Review* 255:1 (1970): 58–65.

Young, Richard E., Alton L. Becker, and Kenneth L. Pike. *Rhetoric: Discovery and Change.* New York: Harcourt, 1970.

AFTERIMAGE

Finished, it's finished, nearly finished, it must be nearly finished.

(Pause.)

Grain upon grain, one by one, and one day, suddenly, there's a heap, a little heap, the impossible heap.

—Clov in *Endgame* by Samuel Beckett

Keep on heaping.

—AZ

Also available from SOUVENIR PRESS

Solutions for Novelists
by Sol Stein
9780285635685 £12.99

Learn how to write a novel from one of the world's great editors.

"Plenty of how-to books are strong on theory – they explain the theory of writing arresting openings, of creating interesting characters and so forth – but Sol Stein's strength is that he demonstrates these things in highly practical terms."
'Writers News'

Solutions for Writers
by Sol Stein
9780285635258 £12.99

How to write non-fiction the professional way.

"Creative writing courses up and down the country are jammed. But everything you need is in this wonderful volume… Stein is a fascinating guide and teacher. This should be required reading for all Booker prize judges and about 90% of published authors."
'Daily Mail'

The Joy of Writing Sex
by Elizabeth Benedict
9780285636422 £9.99

The classic guide to writing sex scenes that also teaches the craft of writing convincing fiction as a whole.

"Read it because it will teach you everything you need to know about writing good fiction, whether your characters are having sex or having breakfast."
Peter Carey, twice a winner of the Booker Prize

Available from all good bookshops, www.amazon.co.uk or www.bookdepository.co.uk